Opera Guide 41

Josephine Barstow as Lady Macbeth, Opera North, 1987. (Photo: Hanson)

Preface

This series, published under the auspices of English National Opera, is made possible by generous sponsorship. We are most grateful for the continuing support of Martini and Rossi Ltd, who have also sponsored the Opera Guides to *Madam Butterfly* and *A Masked Ball*. Their interest enables us to commission and publish new research and up-to-date English performing translations in volumes with a wide circulation which reach opera-lovers all over the world. We hope that, as companions to the opera should be, they are well-informed, witty and attractive.

Nicholas John
Series Editor

41

Macbeth

Giuseppe Verdi

Opera Guide Series Editor: Nicholas John

This guide is sponsored by Martini and Rossi Ltd **MARTINI**

Published in association with
English National Opera

John Calder · London
Riverrun Press · New York

First published in Great Britain, 1990, by
John Calder (Publishers) Ltd,
9-15 Neal Street, London WC2H 9TU

First published in the U.S.A., 1990, by
Riverrun Press Inc., 1170 Broadway,
New York, NY 10001

BRITISH LIBRARY CATALOGUING IN PUBLICATION DATA
Verdi, Giuseppe: *1813-1901*
    Macbeth. - (Opera guide; 41)
    1. Opera in Italian. Verdi, Giuseppe 1813-1901 2. Opera in Italian
    I. Title   II. Series
    782.1'092'4

    ISBN 0-7145-4148-6

LIBRARY OF CONGRESS CATALOGING IN PUBLICATION DATA
Verdi, Giuseppe, 1813-1901
    Macbeth.

    (Opera guide; 41)
    Includes bibliographical references and discography.
    Also contains essays on the opera by Giorgio Melchiori, Harold Powers, and
Michael R. Booth.
    1. Operas—Librettos.   2. Verdi, Giuseppe, 1813-1901.
Macbeth.   I. Piave, Francesco Maria, 1810-1876.
II. Maffei, Andrea, 1798-1885.   III. Sams, Jeremy.
IV. Shakespeare, William, 1564-1616. Macbeth.   V. Title.
VI. Series
ML50.V484M22   1990   782.1'026'8   89-24312

ISBN 0-7145-4148-6 (pbk)

English National Opera receives financial assistance from the Arts Council of
Great Britain.

Typeset in Plantin by Maggie Spooner Typesetting, London NW5.
Printed in Great Britain by The Camelot Press, Southampton.

Contents

List of illustrations ... vi

'Macbeth': Shakespeare to Verdi *Giorgio Melchiori* ... 7

Making 'Macbeth' 'Musicabile' *Harold Powers* ... 13

'Macbeth' and the Nineteenth-Century Theatre *Michael R. Booth* ... 37

Thematic Guide ... 45

A Note on Shakespeare's 'Macbeth' *August Wilhelm Schlegel* ... 51

The Preface in the Ricordi Libretto ... 54

Piave's Intended Preface for the 1847 Libretto ... 56

'Macbeth' *Italian libretto by Francesco Maria Piave*, 1865 ... 59

'Macbeth' *English translation by Jeremy Sams* ... 61

    Act One ... 61

    Act Two ... 71

    Act Three ... 78

    Act Four ... 84

Additional Scenes from the 1847 version ... 91

Discography *David Nice* ... 92

Bibliography ... 96

Contributors ... 96

List of Illustrations

Cover design: Anita Boyd (after Fuseli)
Frontispiece: Josephine Barstow as Lady Macbeth, Opera North, 1987 (photo: Hanson)

p. 9   Scene from the world première of Verdi's 'Macbeth', Teatro della Pergola, Florence, March 1847 (photo: Royal Opera House Archives)

p. 11   Design for the first production of 'Macbeth', 1847 (photo: Giancarlo Costa)

p. 14   Vera Schwarz as Lady Macbeth at Glyndebourne, 1938 (photo: Glyndebourne Archive/Jeremy Debenham)

p. 16   Rehearsal of Carl Ebert's 1938 Glyndebourne production, designed by Caspar Neher (photo: Glyndebourne Archive/Jeremy Debenham)

p. 17   Margherita Grandi as Lady Macbeth, Glyndebourne, 1939 (photo: Glyndebourne Archive)

p. 19   Glyndebourne at the Edinburgh Festival in 1947 with Owen Brannigan as Banquo and George Christie as Fleance (photo: Glyndebourne Archive/Angus McBean)

p. 24   Maria Callas as Lady Macbeth, La Scala, Milan, 1952 (photo: Erio Piccagliani)

p. 28   *Above:* the first production in Munich, 1934, conducted by Knappertsbusch, with Heinrich Rehsemper and Hildegard Ranczak; producer, Oskar Wallek. *Below:* Piero Cappuccilli as Macbeth, Munich, 1985 (photos: Hanns Holdt, Sabine Toepffer)

p. 29   *Above:* the 1967 Munich production by Otto Schenk, designed by Rudolf Heinrich, with Anja Silja as Lady Macbeth. *Below:* the 1985 Munich production by Roberto De Simone, designed by Giacomo Manzù, with Renato Bruson as Macbeth (photos: Rudolf Betz, Sabine Toepffer)

p. 30   Leonie Rysanek as Lady Macbeth, San Francisco, 1957 (photo: SFO)

p. 32   Inge Borkh as Lady Macbeth, San Francisco Opera, 1955 (photo: Robert Lackenbach)

p. 33   William Dooley and Gladys Kuchta as the Macbeths, Deutsche Oper, Berlin, 1963 (photo: Buhs)

p. 38   The Banquet Scene from 'Macbeth', an engraving after Maclise (photo: Mary Evans Picture Library)

p. 41   Pepper's Ghost as illustrated in the nineteenth-century periodical 'Tricks' (photo: Mary Evans Picture Library)

p. 42   Mr and Mrs Charles Kean in Shakespeare's 'Macbeth', Princess's Theatre, London, 1853 (photo: Mander and Mitchenson Theatre Collection)

p. 43   Amy Shuard as Lady Macbeth and Tito Gobbi as Macbeth, Royal Opera House, Covent Garden, 1960 (photo: Houston Rogers/Theatre Museum)

p. 44   Carlo Bergonzi as Macduff at the Met, 1962 (photo: Metropolitan Opera House Archives)

p. 54   Frontispiece for the first edition, 1847 (photo: Royal Opera House Archives)

p. 57   Omar Ebrahim as Macbeth with the witches, in Richard Jones' production, Scottish Opera's Opera-Go-Round, 1987 (photo: Thorburn)

p. 58   Leo Nucci as Macbeth in Claude d'Anna's 1986 film of the opera (photo: Unitel)

p. 60   Lady Macbeth's sleepwalking scene with Pauline Tinsley, Netherlands Opera, 1985 (photo: Jaap Pieper)

p. 77   Renato Bruson and Renata Scotto in Elijah Moshinsky's production for the Royal Opera House, Covent Garden, 1981 (photo: Reg Wilson)

p. 86   Sylvia Sass in Philippe Sireuil's 1987 production for La Monnaie, Brussels (photo: La Monnaie)

'Macbeth': Shakespeare to Verdi

Giorgio Melchiori

Verdi's and Shakespeare's *Macbeth*s are not identical twins. But there could hardly be a case of closer artistic siblings. They were conceived under similar circumstances, at times of great creative stress, when the authors were under pressure to provide the media in which they worked with — what should we call them? — new pretexts for performance. There is a striking analogy between the working conditions of playwrights in Elizabethan England and opera composers in nineteenth-century Italy. Both saw themselves as skilled craftsmen engaged in making a living by providing respectively 'books' (the Elizabethan name for playscripts) and scores to meet the insatiable hunger of contemporary theatres for new plays in the one case, new operas in the other. They saw themselves too, at times, as convicts sentenced to hard labour — Verdi certainly did so, when in 1858 he wrote to Countess Clara Maffei (the former wife of that fine man of letters, Andrea Maffei, to whom Verdi had turned for help, ten years earlier, with the libretto of *Macbeth*): 'From *Nabucco* onwards I have not enjoyed, I may say, a single hour of rest. Sixteen years of *galera* [solitary confinement].'

There is perhaps some exaggeration in this but the production of no less than sixteen major operas — from *Nabucco* in 1842 to *Il trovatore* and *La traviata* in 1853 — in less than twelve years would not have afforded the author many idle moments. His time was spent ransacking past literature and history in search of suitable subject matter, trying to accommodate the requirements of impresarios, the trends of public taste, the availability and peculiar gifts of singers (the real 'subjects' — Verdi calls them *sogetti* — of his operas), and even the censorial whims of the different Italian states in which such operas were to be performed. For instance, in the case of *Macbeth*, while the tolerant Grand Duke of Tuscany, before whom it was first presented, raised no objection, the Hapsburg censors resented disrespectful allusions to the Crown or to an 'oppressed fatherland' so that in Milan the libretto had to be modified accordingly; the Bourbons in Palermo would not hear of regicide on stage, and King Duncan had to be transformed into Count Walfred, a rival general of Macbeth, while in Rome the Pope would stand no nonsense about supernatural solicitings, so that the witches had to be turned into gypsies with their fortune-telling cards.

Shakespeare in Elizabethan England had been faced with similar problems in the search for material, and with censorship, though he was luckier in another respect: as a shareholder in a well-established company, he knew exactly what suited his 'sogetti', that is to say his fellow-actors. He would certainly never have chosen a subject like *Macbeth* had he not known that by 1605 there was a man (not just a boy-actor) in the company capable of filling the exacting role of Lady Macbeth. As for subject matter: more than a decade earlier Shakespeare had extracted from the pages of Holinshed the grim history of Richard III in order to celebrate the redeeming advent of the Tudor dynasty to which the reigning Queen, Elizabeth, belonged. It was only logical, after the advent to the English throne in 1603 of a Stuart, James VI of Scotland, now James I of England and patron of his company of players, to scrutinize the pages of the same historian in order to find the origins of the Stuarts. There he found another grim story, that of Macbeth, the tyrant who had killed Banquo, the forbear of the new dynasty — with the further advantage that such a story would appeal to the new sovereign's interest in daemonology.

Verdi had no monarch to please, only the impresario Alessandro Lanari, who had commissioned a new opera from him to be presented in the Lent season of 1847 in the theatre in the via della Pergola in Florence, under the patronage of His Imperial and Royal Highness the Grand Duke Leopold II of Tuscany. Lanari's main stipulation was that the new opera should belong to a genre as yet unexplored by Verdi, though already a favourite with Florentine audiences, who had applauded the Italian premières of Meyerbeer's *Robert le diable* and Weber's *Der Freischütz*: the *genere fantastico*. Verdi's first pre-occupation was to find a suitable 'fantastic' subject in the literature of the Northern countries where the genre flourished. Yet, being a man of the theatre, he knew that a crucial factor was which singers would be available for the leading roles — as with Shakespeare and his fellow actors, the final choice of subject depended on them. On May 17, 1846, he wrote to Lanari:

> Now that we are perfectly agreed on the fantastical genre for the opera that I have to write for Florence, you must undertake to let me know as soon as you can the *sogetti* [the performers available]: because I have two *argomenti* [plots] in mind, both of them fantastical and very fine, and I'll choose whichever is better suited to the *sogetti*.

The possible *argomenti* soon became three: *Die Ahnfrau* by the popular German dramatist Franz Grillparzer, Schiller's *Die Räuber*, and Shakespeare's *Macbeth*. Verdi reserved Schiller for another occasion (London), and made the choice for Florence depend exclusively on the availability of a good tenor, indispensable for the Grillparzer subject: either Lanari should engage the tenor Gaetano Fraschini or, as the Maesto wrote to him on August 19,

> I don't want to take risks with other tenors, or worry about other singers: thus, I have a mind to tackle a subject in which the tenor is irrelevant. In this case I would absolutely need the following two artists: `[the soprano *Sofia*] *Loewe* and [the baritone *Felice*] *Varesi*.

Although there is no mention in the letter of Shakespeare's play, what is remarkable is the determination with which Verdi insists on securing Varesi for the as yet unnamed role, offering to write to him himself, in spite of the fact that Lanari had under contract another excellent baritone, Gaetano Ferri,

> who is better looking, has a more beautiful voice, and, if you like, is even a better singer, but *in that role* certainly couldn't give me the effect that Varesi would.

The letter is revealing: Verdi knew Shakespeare's play only in the uninspiring prose translation by Carlo Rusconi, but his sense of music and drama was such that, even before starting composition, he knew exactly what kind of voices he needed for the leading roles. Varesi was in fact the creator of the role of Macbeth. As for Lady Macbeth, Verdi at first regretted that Loewe was not available, but he set to work to model the part on the unhandsome soprano that replaced her, Marianna Barbieri-Nini. In the end he was to object when the part was given to the much better looking and more vocally gifted Eugenia Tadolini for a later production at the San Carlo in Naples. Overstating his case as usual in order to get his way he wrote:

> Tadolini is far too gifted to tackle that role! This may perhaps seem absurd to you!! . . . Tadolini has a good and handsome appearance,

*Scene from the world première of Verdi's 'Macbeth', Teatro della Pergola, Florence, March 1847.
(Photo: Royal Opera House Archives)*

while I want Lady Macbeth to be ugly and evil. Tadolini sings to perfection, while I don't want the Lady to sing at all. [But note that he had already composed 'Vieni t'affretta' and 'Trionfai!'] Tadolini has a stupendous voice, clear, limpid, powerful, while I want for the Lady a harsh, strangled, grim voice. Tadolini's voice partakes of an angelic quality, while I want the Lady's voice to partake of the diabolic.

(Letter to Salvatore Cammarano, November 23, 1848)

Fair is foul and foul is fair: the fundamental lesson that Verdi had learned from Shakespeare — even in Rusconi's wretched translation — was that in this case beautiful voices mattered less than dramatic power. Hence his reproaches to the writer of the libretto, Francesco Maria Piave. In letter after letter Verdi insisted that Piave should use fewer words: 'ALWAYS BEAR IN MIND TO USE FEW WORDS, FEW WORDS, FEW, FEW BUT SIGNIFICANT' (September 22, 1846). In the end he asked for help with the last two Acts from Andrea Maffei, who knew *Macbeth* in Schiller's German adaptation. 'Few but significant words' are indeed the main feature of Shakespeare's style in this, by far the shortest of his tragedies. In *Macbeth* Shakespeare counted for 'effect', for the colouring, the atmosphere and dramatic impact, on the power of imagery, the recurrent figures of antithesis and the play of metaphors that add a visionary dimension to the words. Verdi, knowing that the verbal richness of the original would have been largely lost when reduced to libretto form, conceived a score that would more than compensate: it would recreate that visionary dimension through sounds.

He himself sketched out a detailed plan (now lost) of the libretto based on Rusconi's translation. He knew exactly which scenes should be left out altogether — among them the spurious Hecate scene at Act Three, scene 5 — which should be added, compressed, or transposed, which characters and speeches could be dispensed with or conflated. The most significant addition is

9

the chorus of Scottish refugees opening Act Four, immediately followed by Macduff's aria — the only aria for a tenor in the whole opera: this both compensates for the omission of the on-stage murder of Macduff's wife and son, and adds to the drama by making it the tragedy of an oppressed nation. This development would find an immediate response in Italian audiences at a time before the first war of the Risorgimento had taken place.

From the beginning Verdi conceived an important role for the chorus in *Macbeth* as an opera — the three witches become three groups of at least six witches each, and Banquo is killed by a whole army of murderers. As early as October 15, 1846, when the libretto was largely unwritten, Verdi had warned his impresario:

> Here's the outline of *Macbeth* and you'll understand what it is like. You see that I need an excellent chorus: especially the women's chorus must be very good because there will be two witches' choruses of the utmost importance . . . the things that need special care in this production are *Chorus and Machinery*.

This might appear to be a major departure from Shakespeare's play, which can be read as the private tragedy of Macbeth and Lady Macbeth. On the contrary, the power of music reveals the play's fundamental tension: in this exploration of the relationship between two worlds — the world of man, and a world of indefinable forces — the latter can both generate evil (the witches, the murderers) and, when linked with human suffering, become a force for good.

*

It is well known that the text of Shakespeare's *Macbeth* which has survived is in part the work of another hand. Obviously for reasons of spectacle a whole scene — that of the apparition of Hecate at Act Three, scene 5, which is an unwarranted intrusion into the tight sequence of the action — as well as songs and stage effects in the later witches' scene, have been interpolated, probably without the author's approval. Verdi was more fortunate when his opera was subjected, for similar reasons, to similar treatment. With a production of a French version of the opera in view at the Théâtre Lyrique in Paris in 1865, Verdi was asked to extend the witches' scene in Act Three by providing music for a ballet in the Parisian tradition. Verdi agreed, but the introduction of the witches' ballet became the pretext for a radical revision of the whole opera. For the ballet Verdi had to fall back upon the formerly rejected spurious Hecate scene, which was presented as a dumb show — an obvious concession to current taste, like the intrusion of the equivalent scene in Shakespeare's play. What really mattered for Verdi was the chance of making the other changes, which he announced in a tone of self-reproach:

> I have looked through *Macbeth* in order to write the ballet music, but alas! upon reading through the score I have been struck by things that I would not have wished to have found there. In a word, there are several numbers which are either weak or lacking in character — which is even worse . . .
> 1st An aria for Lady Macbeth in Act Two
> 2nd Several passages to rewrite in the Vision of Act Three
> 3rd Rewrite completely Macbeth's aria in Act Three
> 4th Retouch the opening scenes of Act Four
> 5th Rewrite the last Finale, leaving out the death of Macbeth on stage.
> (Letter to Léon Escudier, October 22, 1864)

10

Design for the first production of 'Macbeth', 1847. (Photo: Giancarlo Costa)

These alterations should be assessed in the light of Verdi's reading of the Shakespearean text.

1. In the 1847 version Lady Macbeth's short aria was a cry of triumph upon having convinced her husband to eliminate Banquo; the new extended version suggested by Verdi and discussed in great detail with Piave (letters of December 1864) strikes a new soberer note, by borrowing from Macbeth's meditation on the planned murder, 'Scarf up the tender eye of pitiful day . . .'.

2. The changes in the Apparitions' scene are essentially of a musical nature, intended to link it up with the new witches' ballet to be inserted immediately before it.

3. This is the most interesting of the textual as well as musical changes. Macbeth's aria at the close of the Apparitions' scene, modelled on his monologue at the end of the equivalent scene in Shakespeare — when he seems reduced to the status of a conventional bloody stage tyrant — is replaced by a recitativo and duetto with Lady Macbeth. Their double involvement in the new murder plan suggests that both are possessed by the powers of evil, and is a most effective prelude to the sleep-walking scene. Significantly Verdi insisted to Piave (letter of December 1864) that in writing the text of the duetto he should 'use the thought and even the very words of Shakespeare'; he did not know that the words he wanted preserved were in fact an arbitrary intrusion by Shakespeare's Italian translator Carlo Rusconi.

4. The music of the opening chorus of Act Four was completely rewritten, though the text remained unchanged; the new musical version anticipates the replacement of the last scene of the opera.

5. Both text and music of the last scene were radically changed. Verdi's own careful new wording of the whole is witnessed by the letter to Piave of January 28, 1865. The earlier version included a dying speech for Macbeth which is utterly unShakespearean in spirit. In the new version, as in Shakespeare, Macbeth dies offstage; the final hymn of victory by a multiple chorus is the perfect musical counterpart of Macduff's and Malcolm's closing speeches in the play. Even Verdi's apparently arbitrary inclusion at this point of a chorus of Bards (he carefully explains to Piave: 'The Bards, as you know, followed the armies in those days') contributes to the Shakespearean note of celebration, recalling the chorus of refugees at the beginning of the Act, and containing an implicit homage to the English Bard who first devised the tragedy.

Shakespeare gave Verdi a fresh insight into the nature of drama for music. For this reason Macbeth is so different from all he wrote before and after 1847. He acknowledged it some thirty years later, when, interviewed by the Vienna Neue Freie Presse (June 1875) on Richard Wagner's achievement, he commented: 'I too have attempted the fusion of music and drama, and I did so in Macbeth; but I could not write my own librettos, as Wagner does.' His comment is only partly accurate, since on no other occasion had Verdi contributed so much to the writing of his own libretto — few words but significant, the essence of Shakespeare's music.

Making 'Macbeth' Musicabile

Harold Powers

1. Verdi and Shakespeare

In a memorial essay on Verdi published in 1901, George Bernard Shaw, that
most literate of opera-lovers, quipped:

> the truth is that instead of *Otello* being an Italian opera in the style of
> Shakespear, *Othello* is a play written by Shakespear in the style of an
> Italian opera.... With such a libretto Verdi was quite at home: his
> success with it proves, not that he could occupy Shakespear's plane but
> that Shakespear could on occasion occupy his, which is a very different
> matter.[1]

What Shaw wrote about Shakespeare's *Othello* and Verdi's *Otello* is true of all
the plays Verdi and his librettists made into operas. Verdi wanted for his
musical theatre not a drama for which he would provide background music,
but a play that could be made, to use his own expression, *musicabile*.

Of Verdi's twenty-four operas from *Nabucco* in 1842, his third opera and
first overwhelming success, through to his final triumph in 1893 with *Falstaff*,
nineteen are based on spoken plays of non-Italian origin. The playwrights
represented more than once in the Verdian canon are Victor Hugo,
Shakespeare, Schiller and Antonio Garcia Gutiérrez. If one were also to take
into account plays that Verdi is known to have had in mind but in the end
never made into operas, then Hugo, and above all Shakespeare, would loom
even larger. In addition to the *Macbeth*, *Otello*, and *Falstaff* that Verdi actually
composed, there is first and foremost *King Lear*, whose completed libretto by
Antonio Somma is among Verdi's papers at the family estate of Villa
Sant'Agata.[2] There are two other completed Shakespearean librettos at
Sant'Agata. One is a fully versified libretto of *La tempesta* by Andrea Pannizza
copied out in Verdi's hand, dated 1866. The other is a prose draft libretto in
French called *Rowena* that turns out to be based on *Cymbeline*. *Hamlet* appears
in a list of possible subjects probably drawn up by Verdi in 1849 but when the
subject was actually proposed to him, by Giulio Carcano in 1850, he
demurred.

So Verdi clearly regarded Shakespeare as a playwright who was very
musicabile indeed. But we must remember not only that an Italian opera based
on Shakespeare is not a Shakespeare play in Italian with incidental music; we
must also remember that the Shakespeare Verdi knew is not the Shakespeare
we know. Shakespeare's language came to Verdi, and to his librettists, not in
English but through Italian and French translations, some in prose, some in
verse, some good, some bad. Verdi's knowledge of *Macbeth* at the time of its
composition, for instance, was through the prose translation of Carlo Rusconi
(Padua 1838). And furthermore, Shakespeare's dramas came to Verdi
embedded in a Continental critical tradition rather different from the British
one: not Thomas Rymer or Samuel Johnson, let alone A.C. Bradley or T.S.
Eliot, but rather Schlegel and François-Victor Hugo. Verdi's Shakespeare was
the rallying point of Continental Romanticism (the English critic most nearly
relevant would be Coleridge). The contrast of grotesque and tragic to which
Hugo constantly returned in the prefaces to his seminal plays of the 1830s was
embodied for him in Shakespeare, whom he regularly cited as the antithesis of
the classical unities of the *grand siècle*, the classical monotony of affect and
effect.

Vera Schwarz as Lady Macbeth at Glyndebourne, 1938. (Photo: Glyndebourne Archive/Jeremy Debenham)

We ought not, then, to compare Verdi directly with Shakespeare as we know him. We need to be able to see the play as Verdi saw it, as a nineteenth-century man of the Italian musical theatre saw it, a man who happened to be a great dramatist in his own right, but in a different medium, at a different time, and in a different place. Properly to understand the relationship between Verdi and Shakespeare, we need to be familiar above all with the process of mediation, the way a Shakespeare play becomes a Verdi opera, the way it gets made *musicabile*.

For a play to be *musicabile*, three things were necessary: a palpable ambience, striking characters and, above all, strong situations. Verdi's correspondence with his librettists shows that he chose plays to make into operas because of their potential, in these three domains, for effective music. Once a play had been chosen, the opera was hammered out, in terms of its plot structure, its poetry, and its music. Pierluigi Petrobelli has summarised the relationships in terms of

the interaction of the three main systems — dramatic action, verbal organisation, and music . . .

pointing out that

the articulation of the musical language is already present in the organisation of the libretto. In other words, the verbal structure is determined by the musical structure, and is governed by dramatic principles.[3]

Petrobelli's 'three main systems — dramatic action, verbal organisation, and music' — should be examined two by two rather than one at a time, for the dominant mode of interaction in each of the three possible pairings highlights a different structural plane — background, middleground, and foreground — within the synthesis of the completed opera.

Action is correlated with music on the background plane of formal layout, in a synopsis of the play organised according to the nature and order of large musical numbers: introductions, aria scenes, duet scenes, finales, and so on. The synopsis might be made by librettist, composer, or both, or even by or with the collaboration of some third party. It was in principle a joint effort, in which all parties had to concur in trying to reach a particular public, though Verdi's was the determining voice. For such a synopsis the terms *schizzo, selva,* or *programma* were used. Though no such synopsis for *Macbeth* is known to have survived, from Verdi's letters to Piave of September 4 and 22, 1846, and from another to Tito Ricordi of April 11, 1857, it is known that one was made, and that it was exactly like others known from the period, such as those for *Ernani, Il trovatore,* and *Simon Boccanegra*. Verdi told Ricordi that

I wrote out the whole drama in prose, with divisions into acts, scenes, numbers, etc. etc., then I gave it to Piave to put into verse.[4]

Once the dramatic action has been blocked out in terms of musical numbers, the libretto is organised by the selection and ordering of verse types and of stanza designs within each number, again according to the type of music expected. This is primarily the poet's task, though Verdi often requested a particular metre or even suggested lines and stanzas that became part of the final text.

The foreground is the musical setting of the text itself: specific rhythms and forms, melodies, harmonies, accompaniment figures and instrumental

15

Rehearsal of Carl Ebert's 1938 Glyndebourne production, designed by Caspar Neher. (Photo: Glyndebourne Archive/Jeremy Debenham)

timbres are correlated in detail with specific metres and stanza distribution, with meanings of individual words and moods conveyed in particular phrases, entrances and exits, atmosphere called for in stage directions, and so on. This was composer's business; even so, two of Verdi's poets with independent experience in the musical theatre, Salvadore Cammarano and Arrigo Boito, felt free to make sometimes quite detailed musical suggestions, some of which Verdi followed, and some not.

The ambience and characterisations in Shakespeare were certainly *musicabile*, but most *musicabile* of all were the strong situations, the *contrasti*. As Daniela Goldin has pointed out, for Verdi

> the point of departure is the *posizioni*, the dramatic situations, on the basis of whose initial selection (the scenes) he organized the characters, eliminating those that do not come into the play of *contrasti* and that are not agents or catalysts. From this it follows that the Verdian characters, at least in this case, function not so much as personalities, self-sufficient psychological entities, but rather as events, actor-agents in situations; and it is the situations, not the characters, that determine the oppositions so characteristic of Verdian dramaturgy: Macbeth versus Banquo, Macbeth versus Lady Macbeth; but also Banquo in Act One versus Banquo in Act Two, Lady Macbeth in Act One versus Lady Macbeth in Act Four; while Macbeth, always a prey to external stimuli, is the very symbol of human contradiction, contraposed to himself from one scene to another.[5]

This is the most significant distinction between Verdi and Shakespeare. In Shakespeare's *Macbeth*, as in his *Othello*, it is the deterioration of the principal character that drives the play; in the operas, striking situations in the drama

Margherita Grandi as Lady Macbeth, Glyndebourne, 1939. (Photo: Glyndebourne Archive)

17

become visible and verbal pretexts for striking musical pieces.

Macbeth has an ambience that is palpable indeed. In the 1840s Italian operas were still thought of in terms of genres, though not in the familiar dichotomy of tragic and comic. There was the biblical genre, exemplified in Verdi by his first great success *Nabucco*; there was the historical genre, as seen in his next opera *I Lombardi alla prima crociata*; there were the grand, the passionate, even the bourgeois-realistic genres, though this was in the future for Italian serious opera, in Verdi's *Stiffelio* (Trieste 1849) and *La traviata* (Venice 1853). *Macbeth* belongs to the *genere fantastico*. Verdi was very particular about the stage effects for the fantastic scenes, above all for the three apparitions and the procession of eight kings corresponding with Shakespeare's Act Four scene 1.

There are also striking characters in *Macbeth*. For the most part, they evoke types familiar to Italian audiences of the time. There is a murderous baritone — but Macbeth is a murderous baritone who vacillates, expresses remorse even as he does the deed, brave and timorous by turns, a study in dramatic contrasts easily made musical. There is a *prima donna* who can sing in the bravura style — but Lady Macbeth, like Abigaille in *Nabucco*, is obsessed with power; she is ruthless as Lucrezia Borgia in Hugo's play and Donizetti's opera; yet she finishes in a state of altered consciousness, like poor, mad Lucy of Lammermoor in Donizetti's opera, walking in her sleep like Amina in Bellini's *La sonnambula*. And above all, there are the witches, who collectively constitute the third principal character in Verdi's conception. On February 8, 1865, Verdi wrote in connection with the revision of *Macbeth* made for Paris, that

> the roles in this opera are three and no more than three: Lady Macbeth, Macbeth, and the Chorus of the witches. The witches dominate the drama; everything derives from them; coarse and gossipy in the first act, sublime and prophetic in the third. They are truly a character, and a character of the highest importance.[6]

Macbeth has strong situations, whose *contrasti* could be used as dramatic underpinning for effective, even violent, musical contrasts. Those contrasts, though, are always bound together within the sturdy dramaturgical frameworks of Italian Romantic opera, frameworks of convention that Verdi often modified, distorted, even aborted, but never abandoned; they were, after all, the link to his public, and manipulating audience expectations (either by satisfying or surprising them) was his surest way to success. Some of the most powerful situations have been mentioned. The scene where the witches mediate a confrontation of Macbeth and the three apparitions naturally suggested a further familiar musico-dramatic *topos*, that Frits Noske has called the 'ritual scene', in which everything happens three times, each time at a higher pitch.[7] There are several overlays to its threefold structure, especially in the Paris revision of 1865, but the Shakespearean trinity of witches and apparitions was obviously *musicabile*.

In the Banquet Scene, Shakespeare's Act Three scene 4, there are *contrasti*, between the festivities on the one hand, and Macbeth's reaction to Banquo's ghost on the other. Musically this situation takes the form of a *brindisi* (a drinking song) — another familiar kind of number — prefaced by dialogue of hosts and guests over 'party music' in the vein later exploited for the *Introduzione* in *Rigoletto* and *La traviata*. Here the final cadence of the party music after the first stanza of the *brindisi*, and the final cadence of the second stanza of the *brindisi* itself, are each brutally pushed aside by music of the *genere fantastico*, for Macbeth's reaction to Banquo's ghost. And all this — party

Glyndebourne at the Edinburgh Festival in 1947 with Owen Brannigan as Banquo and George Christie as Fleance. (Photo: Glyndebourne Archive/Angus McBean)

music, *brindisi*, and interruptions — serves to prepare for a majestic *pezzo concertato* halting the action in the traditional manner to conclude a spectacular Finale.

2. Design for a murder

In the autograph of the 1847 version, the opera is divided into sixteen numbers, numbered 1 to 15, with 8½ coming between No. 8 and No. 9. The manuscript copy in Paris with Verdi's autograph replacements and emendations for the 1865 version is divided the same way. The many 1865 foreground changes range from details of harmonisation and instrumentation to recomposition of substantial fragments as in No. 9 (the Act Two Finale), where Macbeth's reactions to Banquo's ghost were replaced. In 1865 on the middleground plane a few movements, while retaining their original musico-dramatic functions within the number (and *a fortiori* within the sequence of numbers), were given new music and sometimes new text too: the set piece after the opening *scena* in No. 7, Lady Macbeth's free-standing *cabaletta* 'Trionfai!', was replaced by the extraordinary aria 'La luce langue'. No. 12, the chorus of Scottish refugees that opens Act Four, has the same words but new music. Most radically, the last half of No. 15 was replaced: the music from the report of Lady Macbeth's death was recomposed and, instead of ending the opera with Macbeth's death song, Macbeth was killed offstage and the opera was ended with a chorus of bards and general Hymn of Victory.

The background plane, however — the relationship and the ordering of Verdi's musical numbers to Shakespeare's plot — is the same in both versions. Table I shows how the sequence in Rusconi's translation of Shakespeare's Act One scene 5 to Act Two scene 3 was refashioned to make four musical numbers for the murder scene in Verdi's Act One. A *schizzo* would be the same in either version, with different descriptive language only needed occasionally within numbers.

19

Table I
A 'schizzo' as Piave and Verdi might have devised it

A 'schizzo' for the musical numbers in the second set of Act One, i.e. 'Antechamber in Macbeth's castle, leading to rooms beyond'. 'SH' stands for the Shakespearean sources and '+' in No. 6 indicates there is material with no Shakespearean warrant.

No. 3. Cavatina Lady Macbeth (SH I.5) Lady Macbeth reads a letter from Macbeth, is overjoyed at the prospect of the throne, but fears Macbeth may not be sufficiently strong-willed for the necessary evil-doing. A servant announces the imminent arrival of the King (accompanied by Macbeth), who will stay the night. Lady Macbeth invokes infernal aid to support her murderous designs.

No. 4. Recitativo (SH I.5, 7) *e marcia* (cf. SH I.6) Macbeth arrives, and Lady Macbeth urges him on to do murder. A rustic march, approaching ever closer, announces the arrival of King Duncan. Accompanied by Banquo, Macduff, Malcolm, Macbeth, Lady Macbeth, and train, the King enters, crosses, and leaves, as the march dies away.

No. 5. Scena e duetto (SH II.1, line 31-end, II.2, I.7) Macbeth imagines a dagger leading him on, sees the night world as filled with evil, hears a bell, resolves to murder the King, goes to do so. Lady Macbeth, entering, hears an owl, then Macbeth's voice within. Macbeth reenters: the murder is done. He is horrified by his deed; she mocks his fears. He will not take the bloody dagger back in to incriminate the guards; she takes it, goes off to do so. He hears knocking at the castle gate. She reenters, urges him to leave before they are discovered, and continues to mock his fears; he is still horrified by what he has done.

No. 6. Finale I (SH II.3, lines 46-89, +) Macduff and Banquo enter. Macduff goes to wake the King; Banquo expresses his foreboding. Macduff returns in horror —Banquo goes to see for himself while Macduff rouses the castle; all come on stage. Banquo returns, announces that the King has been murdered. There is general consternation and invocation of supernatural wrath upon the unknown assassin.

That the number of characters increases as the sequence progresses fulfils a fundamental generic expectation in Italian opera. The first Act would begin with an *Introduzione*. In the second scene of the first Act the prima donna would have an entrance aria, called *cavatina*, to be followed by the entrance of a second principal for a Grand Duet; more characters would then enter, with the action arranged to lead up to an ensemble Finale whose centrepiece would be an impressive *pezzo concertato* at a relatively slow tempo. (See Table II.)

Terms like *cabaletta* and *pezzo concertato* — not to mention 'slow movement' — designate movements *within* whole musical numbers; they are musico-dramatic events on the middleground plane where poetic structure and dramatic structure constitute the primary relationship. Of course this relationship too is ultimately governed by musical expectations, for within numbers as well there were conventions about the relationship between kinds of poetic text and musical movement. These conventions may be followed, bent, or thwarted, but they are not simply ignored.

The Shakespearean sequence of events between Macbeth's entrance in Act One scene 5 and the discovery of the murder in Act Two scene 3 lent itself to the generic expectations of an Aria-Duet-Finale sequence. The omission of Duncan from all but an instrumentally accompanied procession was a decision made at the background level; it avoids any interruption of the sequence, as well as being an economy in casting. Shakespeare's porter scene would similarly have broken the Aria-Duet-Finale progression.

Table II
Generic expectations in Italian Romantic 'melodramma'

Grand Duet		Aria/Cavatina	Central Finale
[0] *Scena*		*Scena*	chorus, ballet, scena, aria, duet, etc.
[1] *Tempo d'attacco*	stanzas dialogue	—	*Tempo d'attacco* [kinetic]
[2] *Adagio/cantabile/Slow movement*		*Adagio*	*Pezzo concertato* [static]
[3] *Tempo di mezzo*		*Tempo di mezzo*	*Tempo di mezzo* [kinetic]
[4] *Cabaletta/Stretta*		*Cabaletta*	*Stretta* [static]

The major distinction within a musical number is between the *scena* and the rest: the *scena* is written in *versi sciolti* (loose verse), the rest in *versi lirici* (lyric verse). *Versi sciolti* are normally unrhymed and enjambed; they are the Italian equivalent of blank verse, though two standard line lengths are used rather than one. Long speeches in *versi sciolti*, however, frequently end with a rhyming couplet, like Shakespearean speeches in blank verse; with some librettists, though hardly ever Piave, rhymes occur sporadically in *versi sciolti*. A *scena* delineates the context out of which movements of alternating confrontation and reflection grow. The expected musical texture for *scena* verse is recitative: the words are declaimed melodically, more or less in the rhythm of speech rather than in strict musical time, intermittently punctuated or accompanied by the orchestra.

Subsequent movements will be in *versi lirici*, which are lines in one metre, rhymed, and normally not enjambed. *Versi lirici* are grouped into stanzas by rhyme pattern. In kinetic movements the lines are broken up but the static movements have stanzas of uniform size, evenly distributed among the characters. The music in both kinds of movement proceeds in strict time — *tempo giusto* — but in different kinds of textural relationship between voice and orchestra. In kinetic movements, the melody lies in the orchestra with the vocal lines superimposed, either lyrically, doubling the orchestral melody, or declaiming.[8] In static movements, it is the voice or voices which carry the musical continuity while the orchestra accompanies.

Kinetic movements prepare static movements by leading up to a revelation, confrontation or event that turns the actors into a *tableau*. Ideally a single word or phrase, a *parola scenica*, 'sculpts the scene'.[9] Once the action has been 'sculpted', a formal set piece is developed as an expression of sentiment or mood.

The expectation is that there will be two static movements, the second more spirited than the first. In duet and aria scenes the tempo *adagio* has been entered for [2] following Basevi.[10] The term *cantabile* is often used. Because of the ambiguities inherent in both *adagio* and *cantabile* to describe a genre, however, the English expression 'slow movement' is preferable.[11]

The static movement [4] is called *cabaletta* (etymology unknown) in aria scenes, *stretta* (tightening) in ensemble Finales, and by either term in Grand Duet scenes. Though it is rarely slower than [2], it is not always fast and noisy.

Between a slow movement and a *cabaletta/stretta* a kinetic *tempo di mezzo* (movement in between), was expected to introduce new action to build to a second stopping point. Shakespeare's Act One scene 5 provided a perfect situation for the *prima donna's cavatina* with *tempo di mezzo*, as well as a striking opening *scena*.

The kinetic movement [1], labelled *tempo d'attacco*, sets up the first static movement in a duet or Finale. In most aria scenes, the *scena* is followed by a static slow movement, though when two or more principals are on stage before an aria, this too may be set up by a *tempo d'attacco*.

Making dividing points and elisions in Shakespeare for the musical movements presented relatively few problems. To get Lady Macbeth's *cavatina* (No. 3) out of Shakespeare's Act One scene 5 the only decision was where to begin the slow movement. In the Finale (No. 6), the exits and entrances that follow the announcement of the murder were replaced by some of Piave's text not based on Shakespeare; this not only simplified the action but, more importantly, provided for a *pezzo concertato*. Providing a motivation and a structure for a static slow movement in the duet (No. 4) was Piave's only serious problem. The dramatic confrontation in the play (from Act One scene 5 through Act Two scene 3) is between resolution and vacillation, whether in Macbeth's mind or between Lady Macbeth's resolution and Macbeth's vacillation. The internal conflict is expressed in two great monologues: 'If it were done when 'tis done' from Act One scene 7, and 'Is this a dagger which I see before me?' from Act Two scene 1. Each monologue is followed — in the former case immediately, in the latter after the murder — by a confrontation with Lady Macbeth, a dialogue on the same theme. Given the decision to express the resolution-vacillation confrontation musically in monologue as well as in dialogue, either would have made a logical sequence for *scena* and *tempo d'attacco*. The musico-dramatic problem in both cases is the same, that there is no obvious pretext to stop the dialogue for a reflective slow movement. The problem is compounded in the second instance by the fact that Macbeth's reentrance after the murder with 'I have done the deed' is the best moment for a *parola scenica* — it became 'Tutto è finito' — but it comes too soon to stop the action and launch a slow movement; it comes before rather than after the two-person confrontation that would have to be used to make the *tempo d'attacco*. The monologue of the 'dagger of the mind', however, with its vivid pictorialism, followed by Lady Macbeth's speech at the beginning of Act Two scene 2 — not to mention the bell 'that summons thee to heaven or to hell' and the hoot of an owl — is not only more suited to the *genere fantastico* but also more *musicabile* than Macbeth's more philosophical monologue. Furthermore the monologue and dialogue in Shakespeare's Act Two are directly linked to the act of murder, as they are not in his Act One.

The problem of how to stop the confrontation for a slow movement, and the related problem of the *parola scenica* occurring before the confrontation rather than as its climax, could not be overcome without manipulating either the Shakespearean text or the generic expectations, and in fact both were manipulated. Piave made an ingenious if obvious amplification of Shakespeare to provide a more formally structured lyrical slow movement, inventing some new text for Lady Macbeth to do so. And Verdi balanced the premature *parola scenica* by making a formal close and a thematic recurrence later on, where neither would normally be expected.

Piave's solution for the slow movement of the duet was to divide the Shakespearean dialogue at the moment where Macbeth stops reporting what was heard and said, or not said — ' "Amen" stuck in my throat' — and starts reporting what he imagined: 'Methought I heard a voice cry "Sleep no more" / ... "Glamis hath murdered sleep, and therefore *Cawdor* / Shall sleep no more: *Macbeth* shall sleep no more".' But however useful this may have been for distinguishing kinetic from static, Lady Macbeth's lines in Shakespeare continue in a thoroughly unreflective manner. In order to give her a matching stanza for the slow movement, Piave simply adapted Macbeth's speeches, as he had versified them, to make Lady Macbeth's response, attaching three verbal parallels that do not exist in Shakespeare to the one that does (Macbeth:

'Methought I heard a voice cry ...' Lady Macbeth: 'Who was it that thus cried?'). To Macbeth's tale of what his voice told him, Lady Macbeth rejoins with a sarcastic parody.

MACBETH

A voice spoke within me, unearthly and hollow:	Allor questa voce m'intesi nel petto:
'Your nightmare has started, but worse is to follow!	Avrai per guanciali sol vepri, o *Macbetto!*
You murdered him sleeping, so sleep you have murdered!	Il sonno per sempre, *Glamis*, uccidesti!
And you, Thane of Cawdor, will not sleep again!'	Non v'è che vigilia, *Caudore*, per te!

LADY MACBETH

But what of the voices you should have been hearing?	Ma, dimmi, altra voce non parti d'udire?
'Macbeth is ambitious, but he is a coward: His work is not finished, he dare not complete it.	Sei vano, o *Macbetto*, ma privo d'ardire: *Glamis*, a mezz'opra vacilli, t'arresti,
The heart of a baby, a vain, boastful boy.'	Fanciul vanitoso, *Caudore*, tu se'.[12]

The parallelism in poetic construction and the contrast in semantic affect are both reflected in Verdi's music. The openings of each first line [5a, b] are unharmonised, with instruments doubling the melody (or even only part of it). The second half of Macbeth's line 'Allor questa voce m'intesi nel petto' is set exactly like the first half; the second half of Lady Macbeth's 'Ma, dimmi, altra voce non parti d'udire?' is harmonised in the upper strings, but like Macbeth's line, it continues in b♭ minor, with the g♭-f of Macbeth's 'voce' in the cellos' bass line.

As for the second lines, the parallelism is most marked in the setting of the first half, and the parallel continues in only slightly less strict form in lines 3 and 4. Macbeth's line is a four-bar phrase stretched to five by a written-out ritenuto, as the opening repeated b♭s are lifted up to rest on c'. His line 3, the 'Glamis' line, has the same musical pattern one tone higher, bringing c' up to d'; his line 4 reverts to an unprotracted four-bar phrase and brings the line up through e♭' and e' to climax at three repeated f''s for '[Cau]dore per [te]'. Lady Macbeth's parody in her own lines 2, 3 and 4 is similarly shaped: the repeated d''s and their slow mordent of the first half of line 2 are matched a tone higher with e♭''s in the first half of line 3; they climax yet another tone higher in her final line 4, with three repeated f''s moving up to g'' for '[Fan]ciul vanito[so]'.

The musical devices linking the settings of their respective stanzas, to sum up, are these: unisons in the respective lines 1 versus harmonised accompaniment in the respective lines 2, 3 and 4; and in each one's stanza those three lines themselves are similarly set, each with a repeated-note figure in the same rhythm, a figure that is repeated twice more in rising stepwise sequence. These parallels in textural and motivic design constitute a musical equivalent of the parallels in the poetic design of the stanzas.

The contrast in the semantic affect for the imagined voices — Macbeth's threatening, Lady Macbeth's mocking — is likewise matched in the music: in the continuing minor mode for Macbeth's imagined voice versus the Major mode for his Lady's parody; and in hammering laden low winds and climactic timpani for Macbeth versus the cellos and clarinet for his Lady.

Maria Callas as Lady Macbeth, La Scala, Milan, 1952. (Photo: Erio Piccagliani)

With such entrances as 'I have done the deed' ('Tutto è finito') and 'Our royal master's murdered' ('È morto assassinato il Re Duncano!') as *coups de théâtre*; with the striking characters of a ferocious yet sometimes indecisive warrior in the title role and an ambitious leading lady who finishes with a mad scene, with contrasting situations which invited adaptation to the expectations of the lyric theatre, and with an ambience so suited to the *genere fantastico* as that provided by the prophecies and apparitions created by a coven of witches, what Bernard Shaw wrote of *Othello* and *Otello* was obviously just as true for *Macbeth* and *Macbeth* forty years earlier:

> With such a libretto Verdi was quite at home: his success with it proves, not that he could occupy Shakespear's plane but that Shakespear could on occasion occupy his.

3. The three principals

The witches

Verdi's twofold characterisation of the witches as alternatively 'coarse and gossipy' and 'sublime and prophetic' had its source in August Wilhelm Schlegel, who was the most significant of the nineteenth-century Shakespearean critics so far as Verdi's *Macbeth* is concerned. Verdi's understanding of the witches came directly out of an excerpt from Schlegel's 'Lectures on Dramatic Art and Literature' that was appended to Rusconi's translation of *Macbeth* (in the Italian translation of Giovanni Gherardini).

> With one another the witches discourse like women of the very lowest class; for this was the class to which witches were ordinarily supposed to belong: when, however, they address Macbeth, they assume a loftier tone: their predictions, which they themselves pronounce, or allow their apparitions to deliver, have all the obscure brevity, the majestic solemnity, of oracles, such as have ever spread terror among mortals.[13]

This can be added to Daniela Goldin's listing of the 'play of *contrasti*' in Verdi's *Macbeth*, and Verdi used the witches' opposed qualities to open his opera. A combination of features makes the tune shown in Example 1A/1 'coarse and gossipy', chief among them the staccato repeated notes, the increasingly odd downward skips on 'pensier', 'lo spo[so]', and 'suo le[gno]', and the out-of-context long note at the bottom of the skip, followed by a sudden doubling of the pace. This musical vulgarity is related to the text, based on the first witch's 'A sailor's wife had chestnuts in her lap' speech. The trills in the melody-doubling upper winds accompanying the witches' twice accented d♯, and the steady staccato chords in the orchestra, though they have no intrinsically vulgar flavour, are appropriately crude at this tempo. The witches' address to Macbeth is a different matter (Example 1A/2). The 'majestic solemnity of oracles' is marked by the slower tempo, by the threefold rising sequence of salutations to Macbeth, and by solemn accompanying chords in middle and lower winds, marked by shuddering strings. It is a paradigmatic instance of a 'ritual scene'.[14]

A similar contrast of coarseness and sublimity, not quite so stark perhaps, but on a far grander scale, is made between the witches' opening chorus in Act Three (Verdi's No. 10) and the scene of the three apparitions (the *tempo d'attacco* of Verdi's No. 11). The witches' chorus is a vulgar 'ritual' scene, a straightforward italianisation of Shakespeare's 'Thrice the brindled cat hath

Example 1A/1

CHORUS OF WITCHES

SOP. 3

Andante sostenuto

Sal – ve o Mac – bet – to, di Gla – mis si – re!
Hail to Mac – beth, the great Thane of Glamis!

SOP. 2

Sal – ve, o Mac – bet – to, di Cau – dor si – re!
Hail to Mac – beth, the new Thane of Caw – dor!

SOP. 1

Sal – ve, o Mac – bet – to, di Sco – zia re!
Hail to Mac – beth, who will soon be King!

Example 1A/2

CHORUS OF WITCHES

Allegro assai moderato

M'è frul – la – ta nel pen – sier
Let the poi – soned chal – ice say

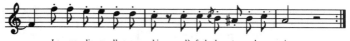

– La mo–glie–ra d'un noc – chier, m'è frul – la – ta – nel pen – sier
– How to hurt the sai–lor's wife, Who is stand – ing in our way.

ma lo spo – so, ma lo spo–so che sal – pò col suo leg –
For her hus – band is a sai–lor on the sea; We will show

no, col suo leg – no af–fo – ghe – rò.
her how ma – li – cious we can be.

mewed ... Double, double, toil, and trouble ...' and so on. But after Macbeth's dialogue with the witches in recitative at the beginning of the next number, the *tempo d'attacco* begins with the witches' invocation of the infernal spirits; it is shown in Example 1B and the tempo, the instrumentation and rhythm in the orchestra, the doubling of the voices with trumpet and clarinet, all support an inexorable triadic rise and fall ('alte regioni ... scendete') that is certainly 'sublime and prophetic'. The scene of the apparitions is a serious 'ritual scene', like their salutations in Act One, but much more complex. And though the witches themselves have little enough to say during the confrontation of Macbeth and the three apparitions, the apparitions in their 'obscure brevity' are, as Schlegel noted, dramatically speaking but emanations of the witches in their 'loftier tone'.

Example 1B

Andante maestoso

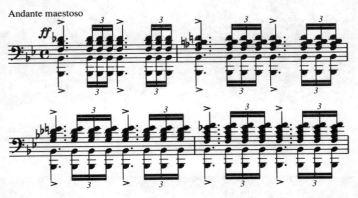

CHORUS OF WITCHES

Dal — le   bas — se e dall — 'al — te   re — gio   ni,
From the   low — est and high — est of   re   —   gions,

spir—ti er — ran — ti,   sa — li — te, scen — de   te!
Let the   spi — rits ap — pear and as — sem   —   ble!

27

Above: the first production in Munich, 1934, conducted by Knappertsbusch, with Heinrich Rehsemper and Hildegard Ranczak; producer, Oskar Wallek. Below: Piero Cappuccilli as Macbeth, Munich, 1985 (photos: Hanns Holdt, Sabine Toepffer)

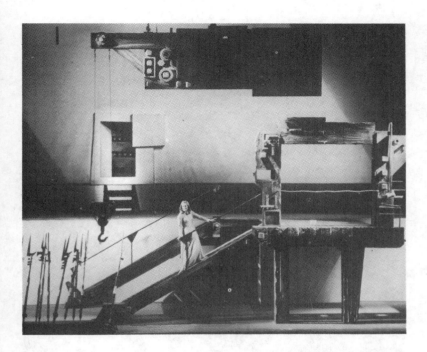

Above: the 1967 Munich production by Otto Schenk, designed by Rudolf Heinrich, with Anja Silja as Lady Macbeth. Below: the 1985 Munich production by Roberto De Simone, designed by Giacomo Manzù, with Renato Bruson as Macbeth (photos: Rudolf Betz, Sabine Toepffer)

Leonie Rysanek as Lady Macbeth, San Francisco, 1957. (Photo: SFO)

Lady Macbeth

Lady Macbeth's personality, for most of the opera as for most of Shakespeare's play, is vividly marked by alternation between public and private ethos, and in her private moods, between ambition for power and apprehension of her husband's will to get it and keep it. At both levels the contrasts are heightened in the opera and its music: the contrast of private versus public by advantageous use of familiar conventions, as in the *cabaletta* 'Or tutti sorgete' in Act One versus the *brindisi* 'Si colmi il calice' [12] in the Act Two Finale (compare Shakespeare's Act Three scene 4); while to her contempt for Macbeth's vacillations is added a tone of mockery, above all in the slow movement of the duet. Her hallucinated final scene is as unprepared in Shakespeare as it is in Verdi, and Shakespeare highlighted the shock of her changed state by casting it in prose. Piave's text matches this effect in that the soliloquy is versified not as an aria properly speaking but as though it were a free-standing *tempo d'attacco*: six quatrains in one verse metre (*ottonario*), grouped in three pairs, with comments from the Doctor and Lady-in-Waiting introduced at the start of stanzas 3, 4, 5 and 6, to make a scene unprecedented in the Verdian canon. The music reflects not only her altered state but a continuity in persona, in giving to her final lyric appearance a musical colour (a *tinta musicale*) that echoes the slow movement of the *cavatina* in Act One (see Thematic Guide [3] and [16]).

Both movements are in Db Major; whether the choice of tonality signifies much in itself is moot, but the common key ensures that the more direct acoustic connection, the similarities in the treatment of the vocal register, will be that much stronger because the very same pitches, the identical qualities of the soprano voice, are involved. Theme [3a] shows the opening phrase (lines 1-2) and [3b] the climax phrase (lines 5-6) of the *Andantino* of her *cavatina*; [16a] and [16b] show the corresponding phrases (lines 1-2 and 5-6) in the first part of the sleepwalking aria. The dominant melodic feature throughout is a consistent disjunction of voice registers, connected midphrase only through the downward fall of the sixth. Moreover, the accompaniment rhythm for the sleepwalking aria echoes that of the *Andantino*: each comprises a bass downbeat followed by a decelerating sequence of repeated afterbeat chords in upper strings. In the sleepwalking aria two figures added to those decelerating afterbeats mark the alteration in Lady Macbeth's state: in the middle strings, a chromatic scale rising through a diminished fifth; in the cor anglais, a descending semitone. Both intervals are familiar symbols in nineteenth-century music, the diminished fifth signifying unnatural evil, the semitone signifying misery. In this context they are readily perceived as complications in Lady Macbeth's musical persona arising from a suppressed guilt as great as that of her husband.

Differing degrees of coherence in Lady Macbeth's discourse in the two passages are signified rhythmically, both in Piave's choice and handling of the verse metres, and in Verdi's musical setting. Piave's *ottonario* verses for 'Una macchia' break midline far more readily than his *settenario* verses for 'Vieni t'affretta'. Verdi exploits the opportunity for disjunction versus continuity (Themes [3] and [16]); note the difference between the low register phrases, the smooth second line of 'Vieni t'affretta', for instance, as against the disjointed first line of 'Una macchia'. Within 'Una macchia', the broken low-register settings of the half-lines 'una macchia', 'è qui tutt'ora', and 'orsù, t'affretta' are in pitiful contrast with the two long lyric phrases that contain the legato drop from upper to lower register, for 'Via ti dico o maledetta' and 'Un guerrier così codardo? / Oh vergogna!'. In 'Vieni t'affretta', to the contrary, there is by and large as much continuity in the low-register phrases as there is elsewhere.

The three sets of paired quatrains in 'Una macchia', with the participation of two onlookers — as opposed to the two uninterrupted quatrains of 'Vieni t'affretta' — led to a fundamental difference of formal dynamic in the musical setting, that emerges only gradually. The first two stanzas of 'Una macchia' Lady Macbeth has all to herself — and the eighteen bars of their music correspond structurally with the twenty bars composed for the whole two-quatrain text of 'Vieni t'affretta'. But where 'Vieni t'affretta' then goes into a long coda, with words from lines 7-8 as the text, 'Una macchia' moves to music for four more quatrains, with contrasting materials, harmonies, and instrumental textures, returning to the principal subject in various keys, and so on. The formal openness of the latter is apparent in the relative amount of text repetition in it, and the corresponding proportions of musical extension to musical substance. More than half of 'Vieni t'affretta' is devoted to purely musical extension or preparation — as befits a static movement. 'Una macchia' is 68 bars long, and the last six constitute an instrumental coda to the scene rather than just to the aria, in that they return to music not heard since the orchestral prelude and *scena*. Text repetitions amount to only about sixteen bars, no more than a quarter of the whole aria. There is plenty of musical development in 'Una macchia', but most of it is done with fresh text, as befits a movement that is truly kinetic — sleepwalking notwithstanding.

Macbeth
Macbeth's musical persona is both too complex and too simple to be dealt with so summarily — too complex in that his moods and music shift frequently and violently, too simple in that they are almost always reactions to external forces, parts of a *contrasto*, whether with the supernatural or with his Lady, or

Inge Borkh as Lady Macbeth, San Francisco Opera, 1955. (Photo: Robert Lackenbach)

William Dooley and Gladys Kuchta as the Macbeths, Deutsche Oper, Berlin, 1963. (Photo: Buhs)

with both at once (in the banquet scene), or with his enemies (in Act Four). His persona is reflected in the *Preludio*, whose subjects are drawn from instrumental music associated with those forces in their most unnatural forms: from the music for the witches and their apparitions in Act Three (with a single flourish from their music in Act One); and from Lady Macbeth's sleepwalking in Act Four. Macbeth himself is given no such obvious characterising music of his own, and in the 1865 version of the opera it is only in his part of the *scena* before the duet — the dagger monologue — and in his Act Four slow movement 'Pietà, rispetto, amore' that we encounter him alone, in the way we come to know Lady Macbeth in her three extended aria scenes.[15] In the 1847 *Macbeth* the protagonist is much more fully developed, and he fully holds his own with the *prima donna*, with a *cabaletta* 'Vada in fiamme!' ending Act Three and a sort of *cabaletta* 'Mal per me' ending the opera.[16] Both were replaced for Paris in 1865, the one with a duet *alla cabaletta* with Lady Macbeth, the other by the triumph of Malcolm and Macduff, as in Shakespeare, and two choruses.

'Pietà, rispetto, amore', with its *scena*, uses most of Macbeth's penultimate moment of reflection in the play (Act Five scene 3). It is a pathetic slow movement, of a familiar cast; in 1847 this constituted the *scena* and slow movement of a single long aria scene for Macbeth, with an elaborate *tempo di mezzo* and a concluding set piece only subliminally perceivable as a *cabaletta*. In 1847, therefore, Macbeth dominated the opera after the sleepwalking scene to the end. In the autograph the sequence is called 'No. 15: scena, battaglia, e

33

morte di Macbet'; the vocal part sent by Verdi on February 4, 1847 to Felice Varesi, the first Macbeth, is headed 'Scena, aria e morte di Macbet'. In the letter accompanying it Verdi referred to the whole sequence in the singular, as 'questa scena finale' and 'l'ultimo pezzo', and he also alluded to its individual lyric movements, as 'un Adagio in re b', 'l'intermezzo', and 'la morte'.[17] The 'Adagio' is of course 'Pietà, rispetto, amore', which was retained unchanged, with its *scena*, in 1865. The 'intermezzo' begins with the report of Lady Macbeth's death and Macbeth's 'tale told by an idiot' and continues with the report that Birnam Wood is on the move, both *decasillabi* passages; a change of set to the battlefield brings in two lines of *ottonari* for Malcolm, and music for the battle. Up to this point the text of the 'intermezzo' remained the same for 1847 and 1865, though the music was increasingly recomposed. For Macbeth's fight with Macduff, the 1847 text continues with lyric verse, in *settenari*; in 1865, their dialogue is in *versi sciolti*, thus breaking the poetic continuity.

In 1847 the fight concludes on stage, with Macbeth mortally wounded. Then comes the non-Shakespearean 'Mal per me che m'affidai / Ne' presagi

The 1847 aria 'Mal per me'

Example 2: 1847

MACBETH

Adagio

dell'inferno' in *versi ottonari*, set to twenty bars of *Adagio* in f minor; a ten-bar *Allegro* for Malcolm, Macduff and chorus concludes the opera.[18] That 'Mal per me' acts as a sub-genre of *cabaletta*, once noted, is undeniable. The slow anapaest rhythms in the accompaniment (see Example 2) project a double image. They hammer out the familiar *topos* that Frits Noske called 'the musical figure of death'[19] and they echo a *cabaletta* accompaniment that is normally heard at a fast tempo.

From a reference in that letter of February 4, 1847, urging Varesi that 'Macbeth mustn't die like Edgardo, Gennaro, etc.', we may even infer that Verdi himself thought of 'Mal per me' as a quasi-*cabaletta* for the dying protagonist, for the deaths of Edgardo and Gennaro form the conclusion of multi-movement final numbers in Donizetti's *Lucia di Lammermoor* and *Lucrezia Borgia* (in the 1840 Milan version that Verdi would have known). Edgardo's 'Tu che a Dio spiegasti l'ali' is a straightforward *cabaletta* in moderate tempo; Gennaro's 'Madre, se ognor lontano' is a 29-bar through-composed *Larghetto* followed by a nineteen-bar *Allegro* outburst from Lucrezia and the orchestra.

Shaping the end of the opera in 1847 as an aria scene — that is, framing the action from the report of Lady Macbeth's death to Macbeth's defeat by Macduff by two set pieces for Macbeth — provides a cohesion by the evocation of familiar conventions. That cohesion was lost in the 1865 revision, whatever may have been gained by a closer approximation to Shakespeare. Also lost was the dominant presence of the protagonist, who simply fades offstage, fighting Macduff the while.

The elimination of Macbeth's 1847 solo *cabaletta* 'Vada in fiamme' at the end of Act Three and the non-Shakespearean reappearance of Lady Macbeth do less damage to the title role quantitatively than the changes to the end of Act Four (Macbeth at least remains on stage to the end of Act Three), but they weaken the coherence of the Act in the same way. The Act was originally conceived as a gigantic aria scene for Macbeth (No. 11 in the autograph), preceded by a scene-setting chorus for the witches (No. 10 in the autograph); for that purpose Shakespeare's Act Four scene 1 needed no structural changes whatever. As already noted, the 'ritual scene' of the witches with their three apparitions in confrontation with Macbeth serves as *tempo d'attacco*. The slow movement of the expanded aria scene is Macbeth's 'Fuggi, regal fantasima'; the phrase structure of the text setting is absolutely regular throughout, but in the first quatrain it is interrupted several times by offstage music for the eight kings; the second quatrain is set, with neither instrumental nor scenic interruption, as 'proper *cantabile*' as Verdi put it in another letter to Varesi.[20] This music too was considerably retouched in 1865 but not changed in essentials. The chorus of witches 'Ondine e Silfidi' and the ballet of aerial spirits, unchanged in 1865, serves as a *tempo di mezzo* between the slow movement and the final static movement, 'Vada in fiamme', a *cabaletta* only slightly modified from the conventional design.[21] In 1865, 'Vada in fiamme' was replaced by a *cabaletta*-like duet movement for Macbeth and Lady Macbeth ('Ora di morte'), preceded by a short *scena* in which Macbeth repeats what we have just heard the apparitions tell him, an uncharacteristic redundancy necessitated by the introduction of Lady Macbeth for a *cabaletta a 2*. The structural cohesion of Act Three — depending on the conventions of an aria scene — was already stretched to the limit in 1847; the new final scene with Lady Macbeth breaks that cohesion so that this Act Three, like the last part of Act Four, is now heard as a series of separate pieces, rather than as a single complex musico-dramatic event.

Notes

1. G.B. Shaw, 'A Word more about Verdi', in *The Anglo-Saxon Review* 8 (March 1901), 221-29.

2. See G. Schmidgall, 'Verdi's *King Lear* project', *19th-Century Music* 9 (1985), 82-101 for a valuable summary of the libretto in relation to Shakespeare.

3. P. Petrobelli, 'Music in the theatre: à propos of *Aida* Act III' in *Themes in Drama 3: Drama, dance and music* (Cambridge UP 1980).

4. The letters may be seen in *Verdi's Macbeth: a Sourcebook*, ed. Rosen and Porter (New York 1982). The *selva* for *Ernani* (by Piave and Mocenigo) is in the Introduction to the Critical Edition of *Ernani* edited by C. Gallico. J.N. Black has published the text of Cammarano's *programma* for *Il trovatore* in *Studi verdiani 2* (Parma 1983). D. Goldin has reedited Verdi's prose summary for *Simon Boccanegra* in the programme for the Maggio Musicale 1989.

5. D. Goldin, 'Il *Macbeth* verdiano' in *La vera fenice* (Turin, 1979, 1985), 245-6.

6. *Sourcebook*, 99.

7. F. Noske, 'Ritual scenes' in *The Signifier and the Signified: Studies in the operas of Mozart and Verdi* (The Hague 1977), 241-70.

8. A. Basevi distinguished these two sub-types of texture as *parlante armonico* and *parlante melodico* in his *Studio sulle opere di Giuseppe Verdi* (Florence 1859), 30-32.

9. Verdi's famous expression is often described ambiguously or erroneously. Verdi used *parola scenica* to denote the word or words that *launch* a set piece — that is, precede it — not the ones that begin it.

10. Basevi op. cit., 191.

11. For the crucial distinction of textural, temporal and formal designations, and for much more besides, I am indebted to the unpublished 1975 Princeton University doctoral dissertation of Robert Moreen, *Integration of text forms and musical forms in Verdi's early operas* (University Microfilms International, UM 76-20782).

12. F. Degrada has shown that a few changes were made in these stanzas when Maffei was touching up Piave's libretto (*Sourcebook*, 163-4 and 317), but they do not affect the basic concept, whereby Lady Macbeth's stanza is a sarcastic parody of Macbeth's, similarly marked by the three names. I have italicised the names to show the parallelism of the verses.

13. *Sourcebook*, 347.

14. Cf. Noske op. cit., 245-7.

15. Lady Macbeth's 1865 Act Two aria 'La luce langue' replaced her 1847 *cabaletta* 'Trionfai!' (*Sourcebook*, 488-91). See page 91.

16. See p. 92.

17. For Verdi's letter to Varesi of February 4, 1847, and a facsimile of the first page of the vocal part he sent, see *Sourcebook*, 41-2.

18. See p. 92.

19. Noske, op. cit., 171-214. I am much indebted to Professor Daniel Taddie of Bethel College (oral communication) for his insightful observation of the double function of the accompaniment rhythms in 'Mal per me'.

20. *Sourcebook* 36 (late January, 1847).

'Macbeth' and the Nineteenth-Century Theatre

Michael R. Booth

Although Verdi knew Shakespeare's *Macbeth* (in Italian translation) and made many efforts to bring Piave's libretto closer to what he believed to be the original text, he had never seen Shakespeare's play on the stage before the Florence première in March, 1947. (He did see it in London three months later.) There were several Italian translations of Shakespeare but no tradition of playing Shakespeare in Italy; the first Italian production of *Macbeth* occurred two years after the first production of the opera. Later, Shakespeare in Italian became part of the repertory of the Italian tragedians Ernesto Rossi and Tomasso Salvini, and *Macbeth* was played extensively in Italy and abroad on tour by Adelaide Ristori, the greatest Italian actress before Eleonora Duse.

Yet the elements of spectacle and fantasy which Verdi stressed in *Macbeth* — supernaturalism, witches, aerial spirits — had a long history in English productions of *Macbeth* and were essential aspects of the nineteenth-century staging of the play, as well as being integral to European production styles in the first half of the century. Verdi may have had no experience of *Macbeth* on stage before the première, but he was certainly aware of, and was part of, the climate of visual display in the theatre of his time.

The element of staging in the opera that most lent itself to spectacular treatment was the supernatural. *Macbeth* in particular among Shakespearean tragedies had long carried the baggage of supernaturalism in performance, and when in England Restoration stage machinery and the vogue of adaptation to prevailing taste were applied to *Macbeth*, supernaturalism became spectacle. Verdi's singing and dancing witches had been a feature of *Macbeth* since Thomas Middleton's Elizabethan interpolation of the Hecate scene and Sir William Davenant's adaptation of 1674, when it is probable that Matthew Locke or William Purcell provided music for them. They survived a long time: Henry Irving's *Macbeth* at the Lyceum in 1888 used a 'Flight of Witches' numbering some fifty or sixty, and much spectacle, with fire glimmering on the mountain rocks, the sky dripping blood, and atmospheric mist a-plenty. The fact that Irving's staging closely resembled his staging of the Brocken scene, or witches' sabbath, in his *Faust* of three years earlier, shows how nineteenth-century producers with the right equipment and stage facilities felt obliged to make the supernatural as spectacular as possible. *Macbeth* was known for this kind of spectacle, especially by the gallery audience. A London costermonger told the investigative journalist Henry Mayhew in the 1850s that he and his mates would like *Macbeth* better 'if it was only the witches and the fighting.' A Punch-and-Judy man interviewed by Mayhew knew the play as *Macbeth and the Three Dancing Witches*.

The form of nineteenth-century drama in which the supernatural was strongest was melodrama. The so-called Gothic melodrama originated in France, influenecd by the English Gothic novel of Horace Walpole and Ann Radcliffe and by the *Sturm und Drang* tragedy of Goethe and Schiller. Melodrama was the expression of the Romantic movement in the popular theatre: in dramatic content, acting style, setting, colour, intensity and sensation. The Gothic variety of melodrama specialised in gloomy castles and equally gloomy tyrants, ruins, wild moorlands and mountains, villainous robber chiefs, noble bandits, virtuous woodsmen and peasants, fleeing heroines with their golden hair down, and ghosts. Before *Macbeth*, Verdi used

The Banquet Scene from 'Macbeth', an engraving after Maclise. (Photo: Mary Evans Picture Library)

the noble bandit in *Ernani*; and his first opera after *Macbeth*, *I Masnadieri*, was a version of Schiller's *Die Räuber*, the classic *Sturm und Drang* tragedy of alienation from an oppressive and corrupt society and the ennobling of violence as a solution for social and personal ills. With its forest setting, Gothic architecture and passionate assertion of man's right to liberty, *Die Räuber* was a strong influence on French Romantic drama and melodrama. Verdi's *Ernani* was an adaptation of Victor Hugo's revolutionary tragedy of 1830, which caused a riot at its first performance and shattered the monolith of classicism in the French theatre.

As for the settings, the standard Gothic landscape was designed to arouse fear and foreboding in the audience. The witches' wood and the dark cavern of Verdi's *Macbeth* have a similar function to the setting of, say, an English melodrama of 1820, *The Warlock of the Glen*, in which one scene is 'the moor at midnight. In the background are the ruins of an abbey surrounded by a few withered tress — the wind is heard at intervals, and the thunder is dying away in the distance. Stage dark.' The last scene of *The Gambler's Fate, or The Hut on the Red Mountain* (1827) is set in 'a ravine, running between a tremendous range of rocky precipices' and illuminated by 'the moon struggling through a stormy sky — the storm rages terrifically — thunder, lightning, and rain.' A melodrama of 1813 set in Ireland, *Suil Dhuv the Coiner*, is similarly *Macbeth*-like in its atmospheric landscape: 'A Druidical circle of rude stones. Lowering, low horizon all round, with flickering lightning breaking through clouds at intervals. A heavy, red full moon, but only half seen, rising slowly and occasionally obscured.'

Storm and tempest characterise Gothic melodrama and Romantic tragedy as much as do remote and blasted landscapes. The authors of these plays knew *Lear* and *Macbeth*. Verdi and Wagner also liked a good storm. The dramatic equivalent of the operatic storm raged in *The Gambler's Fate* and in *The Foundling of the Forest* (1809), in which the hero is pursued by assassins in 'another part of the forest more entangled and intricate — the tempest becomes violent — alternate lightning and utter darkness.' The quintessential forest of Gothic melodrama, the dreaded fastness of evil, is seemingly lit only by lightning.

Reinforced by lighting and sound, the supernaturalism of melodrama was theatrically striking. The first half of the nineteenth century was the last great age of the stage ghost, which appeared in its 'grand finale' in Dion Boucicault's *The Corsican Brothers* of 1852, wherein the spectre of a murdered twin rises mysteriously through the stage, drifting from right to left, to reveal his killing to his distant brother. The ghost of Banquo and the apparitions of the witches' cavern are matched by a generation of spirits in the Gothic melodrama, which glories in spectres and monsters of all kinds, from the phantom bleeding nun of *Raymond and Agnes* (1809) to the first stage vampire in a melodrama of 1820, *The Vampire* (set, rather oddly, in the Hebrides), and ghostly bride of *Alonzo the Brave* (1826), in which the poisoned Imogine rises from the tomb to claim her faithless Alonzo, having previously prevented his marriage to another by appearing at the altar, somewhat alarmingly 'enveloped in a luminous vapour'.

The European stage of the first half of the nineteenth century was more than accustomed to the spectacular presentation of the supernatural. It was also accustomed to the pictorialisation of romantic fantasy. Verdi's *Macbeth* must be placed in the context of the contemporary vogue for fairies and spirits. 'Cult' would perhaps be a better word. It developed throughout Europe from the 1820s to '40s, and in the latter decade — the decade of Verdi's opera —

was at its peak. Hans Christian Andersen was first translated into English in the 1840s; the Brothers Grimm had been translated in the 1820s. The two spirit ballets *La Sylphide* and *Giselle* first appeared in 1832 and 1841; Wagner wrote *Die Feen* in 1834 and Lortzing's *Undine* was first performed in 1845. Paris began to specialise in elaborately produced *folies féeries*, and fairies predominated in Victorian pantomime. It was no coincidence that the 1840s saw the traditional harlequinade scenes of pantomime, which had dominated the genre during the Regency and for some years afterwards, dwindle in number and importance in relation to the fairy and spectacle-filled opening scenes. Not surprisingly, the stage magician was enormously popular at this period, performing his wondrous illusions before audiences of thousands. The fondness for magicians also extended to music-hall audiences in Britain, where magic earned a prominent place on the bill. Verdi's witches would have felt completely at home as 'illusionists' on the nineteenth-century stage. It was only at the last minute that Verdi abandoned the idea of using the fantasmagoria — a French invention based on the magic lantern — for producing the three apparitions at the Florence première. Even popular science could serve the cause of showmanship and the theatre ghost. Pepper's Ghost ('Professor' Pepper was a director of the Royal Polytechnic in London), a supernatural effect produced by mirrors, which found its way from the lecture hall to the theatre, was invented in 1862 and was therefore unavailable for Verdi's *Macbeth*.

The ingenious optics and mechanics of Pepper's Ghost and the fantas-magoria provided ways of reproducing the spirit world in realistic visual images, while the magic lantern was widely used as a means of back projection, frequently for huge images of spirits or angels. Whether historical or contemporary, the environment had to be recreated visually for the edification of audiences. This was achieved by skilful scene-painting and, in the better theatres, an imaginative use of gaslight and limelight. The actor or singer became part of a three-dimensional pictorial composition. This pictorialising of the supernatural or the actual, the unwillingness to trust to the spoken word and the imagination of the spectators, was perhaps the most remarkable feature of nineteenth-century staging.

Not only did the scenic wonders of pantomime express a lavishly romantic fairy world, but Shakespeare came in for the same treatment. Madame Vestris' revival of *A Midsummer Night's Dream* at Covent Garden in 1840 heavily stressed the play's magical elements, especially in Act Five, setting a precedent for major productions of the play for the rest of the century, including Samuel Phelps' at Sadler's Wells in 1853, Charles Kean's at the Princess's in 1854, and Beerbohm Tree's at Her Majesty's in 1900. Although it presents fewer opportunities for fairy spectacle, *The Tempest* was handled in much the same way. The last scene of *The Merry Wives of Windsor* received this type of treatment from Madame Vestris' 1840 revival to the end of the century.

Indeed, Shakespeare lent himself admirably to the art of the painter and the book illustrator as well as to the theatre, and the two are intimately connected. Paintings of Shakespeare's plays decorated Royal Academy exhibitions for generations; especially popular were *A Midsummer Night's Dream* and *The Tempest*. Titania and Oberon and their attendants in the former, Ariel and the spirits of the isle in the latter, were the almost exclusive concern of the painters of these plays, among whom were numbered artists like Richard Dadd, Joseph Noel Paton, Edwin Landseer, and John Millais. Somewhat earlier John Henry Fuseli had produced powerfully grotesque paintings of *A Midsummer Night's Dream,* and both Fuseli and John Martin painted *Macbeth,* the latter in 1820,

Pepper's Ghost as illustrated in the nineteenth-century periodical 'Tricks'. (Photo: Mary Evans Picture Library)

showing Macbeth and Banquo confronting the witches in a vast and desolate landscape. Illustrated editions of Shakespeare proliferated from 1805, with the folio edition of John Boydell and the ten-volume Rivington edition using engravings after Fuseli's drawings. Productions of Shakespeare were 'illustrated' in the same manner as the editions, with pictorialisations of moments in the text or even lengthy visual interpolations of scenes which Shakespeare only described, such as the Battle of Actium in productions of *Antony and Cleopatra* and the entry of Bolingbroke and Richard into London in Charles Kean's *Richard II* in 1857. The moving panorama further illustrated the text. The painter Clarkson Stanfield provided William Charles Macready with panoramas for his 1839 Covent Garden *Henry V* of the voyage of the fleet from Southampton to Harfleur and the Field of Agincourt. It was, incidentally, Macready's *Macbeth* (without a panorama) that Verdi saw in London in 1847.

Thus the relationship between stage production and painting or book illustration was a close one. In England at least, scene painters went on to establish reputations as easel artists, such as — in the first half of the century — Stanfield and David Roberts, both of whom painted scenery for Drury Lane, and David Cox, a scene-painter on the Birmingham theatre circuit. In no other period were the arts of painting and theatre closer; in no other period were the pictorial values of a production considered of such importance.

An interesting aspect of Verdi's wishes for the production of *Macbeth* is his instruction to the designer Perrone that *Macbeth* was to be set specifically in eleventh-century Scotland; Verdi had taken the trouble to check the dates of

Mr and Mrs Charles Kean in Shakespeare's 'Macbeth', Princess's Theatre, London, 1853.
(Photo: Mander and Mitchenson Theatre Collection)

Macbeth's reign. The concern for accuracy of period in costumes, scenery and properties is characteristic of the first half of the nineteenth century, especially in London. It was, after all, a period of archaeological discovery, from the Elgin Marbles to the excavations at Nimrud and Nineveh. These discoveries, made readily accessible to an eager public through the new illustrated magazines, caught the popular imagination and greatly influenced the theatre. The growing interest and pride in British history, the fascination with how people lived and behaved in the past, coincided — not accidentally — with the interest in archaeology. Paintings of scenes from British history poured on to the market and were frequently exhibited at the Royal Academy.

In the theatre, Covent Garden had done a *King John* in 1823 in which costumes and properties, as authentic as research could make them, were designed by the antiquarian-minded J.R. Planché. This was followed by an equally archaeological first part of *Henry IV* in 1824; both were set in their actual historical periods. Macready gave further impetus to the archaeological movement with his *King John* in 1842. Charles Kean's *Macbeth* of 1853 was firmly placed in the eleventh century, and it was the first of his historically scrupulous Shakespearean revivals to be accompanied by a lengthy scholarly disquisition in the playbill, which cited a long list of authorities in support of the historical accuracy of the production. Archaeological zeal continued to be a force in the theatre for generations, not only in Shakespeare, but in any sort of play set in a particular period. Concomitantly, many English painters worked on archaeological lines, such as William Holman Hunt and Lawrence Alma-Tadema. This approach lent itself to stage spectacle: it was the elaborate procession or the palace banquet that interested managers, not the mean street or the authentic hut.

Thus Verdi's *Macbeth* is inseparable, not only from its cultural milieu but also from the major theatrical traditions and production styles of the first half of the nineteenth century. These traditions were highly romantic in nature, and in lavish and sometimes historically recreative stage pictures glorified the supernatural, the fantastic, and the spectacular. It is these traditions and styles that find operatic expression in Verdi's *Macbeth*.

Army Shuard as Lady Macbeth and Tito Gobbi as Macbeth, Covent Garden, 1960. (Photo: Houston Rogers/Theatre Museum)

Carlo Bergonzi as Macduff at the Met, 1962. (Photo: Metropolitan Opera House Archives)

Thematic Guide

Many of the themes from *Macbeth* have been identified in the articles by numbers in square brackets, which refer to the themes set out in these pages. The themes are also identified by the numbers in square brackets at the corresponding points in the libretto, so that the words can be related to the musical themes.

[3b]

LADY

Di Sco - zia a te, a te pro - met - to - no
The time has come: you must as - cend the __ throne...

le pro - fe - tes - - se il tro - - no...
It was fore-told; ____ it is yours ____ a - lone...

[4a]

MACBETH

con voce soffocata e lento   Allegro

(Orch.)

Tut - to è fi - ni - to!
Now it is o - ver!

p

[4b]

MACBETH

sotto voce

Fa - tal mia don - na! un mur - mur - e, com'
Did you not hear it, a mourn - ful sigh..., a

io, non in - ten - de - - sti?
strange un - earth - ly shriek - ing?

[5a]

MACBETH

Andantino

p

Al - lor que - sta vo - ce m'in-te - si nel pet - to:
A voice spoke with - in me, un-earth-ly and hol - low,

[5b]

LADY

Ma, dim - mi, al-tra vo - ce non par - ti d'u - di - re?
But what of the voi - ces you should have been hear-ing?

46

[6]

MACBETH

a voce spiegata

Co—m'an — ge — li d'i — ra, ven—det — ta tuo—nar — mi, u–
Like an — gels with wings made of ven — geance and thun — der, The

— drò di Dun—ca — no le san — te vir — tù.
King will be praised to the Hea — vens a — bove.

[7]

LADY

Presto

p

Vien! vien al — tro — ve, ogni so — spet — to ri — mo—
Quick! We must seem a — bove su — spi — cion. You must

— v'iam dal — l'uc — ci — so — re;
find your for — mer cou — rage.

[8]

ACT ONE FINALE
CHORUS

Adagio

fff

Schiu—di, in—fer — no, la boc — ca ed in — ghiot — ti
Hell is ga — ping in hor — ror and ter — ror

[9]

LADY

legato e cupo

La lu — ce lan — gue, il fa — ro spe — gne-si
Day — light is fad — ing, fire, in the fir — ma-ment,

[10]

CHORUS OF MURDERERS

sotto voce ed assai staccato

Spar — ve il sol, la not — te or re — — — gni
See how soon the sun has left the sky

47

[11]

BANQUO

Adagio

Co - me dal ciel pre - ci - - pi - ta
Black is the night, as black as death,

l'om - bra più sem - pre o - scu - - ra!
dark gloo - my clouds sur - round me!

[12]

LADY *Brindisi*

Allegretto

Si col - mi il ca - li-ce di vi - no e - let - to;
Come fill your glas - ses with wine and glad - ness;

[13]

ACT THREE DUET
MACBETH

Allegro assai

O - - ra di mor - te e di ven - det - ta,
Now is the hour of re-venge and mur - der.

[14]

CHORUS OF SCOTTISH REFUGEES

Andante sostenuto

Pa - tria op-pres-sa! Pa - tria op-pres-sa! il dol - ce
Land of tor - ture! Land of ter - ror! Be-lov - ed

no - me, no, di ma - dre a-ver non puoi,.... ____
mo - ther, hear your sons and daugh - ters cry. ____

[15a]

MACDUFF

Adagio

con espressione melanconica

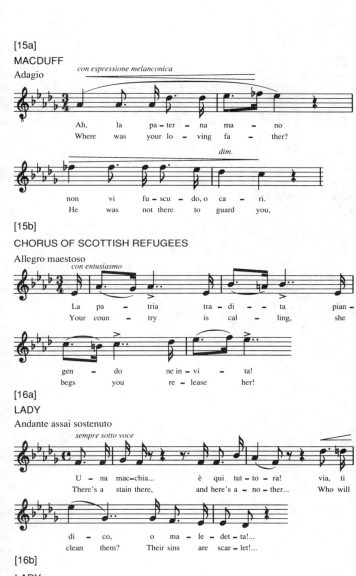

Ah,	la	pa - ter - na	ma -	no
Where	was	your lo - ving	fa -	ther?

dim.

non	vi	fu - scu - do, o	ca -	ri.
He	was	not there	to	guard	you,

[15b]

CHORUS OF SCOTTISH REFUGEES

Allegro maestoso

con entusiasmo

La	pa -	tria	tra - di - - ta	pian -
Your	coun -	try	is cal - ling,	she

gen -	do	ne in - vi -	ta!
begs	you	re - lease	her!

[16a]

LADY

Andante assai sostenuto

sempre sotto voce

U - na mac-chia...	è qui tut - to - ra!	via, ti
There's a stain there,	and here's a - no - ther...	Who will

di - co,	o ma - le - det - ta!...
clean them?	Their sins are scar - let!...

[16b]

LADY

spiegata

Un guer-rier	co - si	co - dar - do?	Oh, ver-
Not a sol - -	dier but	a co - ward.	Oh, it's

go -	gna!...	Or - sù,	t'af - fret - ta!...
shame -	ful!...	Come on,	take cou - rage!...

[17]

MACBETH

Andante sostenuto

Pie – tà,	ri – spet – to, a – – mo – – re,
When you	are ____ old and ____ full of tears,

[18]

CHORUS OF BARDS

Allegro

Mac – beth, ____	Mac–beth ov' – è?	do –
Mac – beth, ____	Where is Mac–beth?	Who

v'è ____	l'u-sur – pa – tor?...
dared ____	to steal the crown?...

A Note on Shakespeare's 'Macbeth'

August Wilhelm Schlegel
translated by Andrew Porter

To Carlo Rusconi's translation of Shakespeare's Macbeth *(Turin, 1838), the principal source of Verdi's libretto, was appended the following 'Nota al Macbeth' taken from August Wilhelm Schlegel's celebrated and influential* Course of Lectures on Dramatic Art and Literature, *delivered in Vienna in 1808 and published, with additions, in 1809 and 1811. Schlegel's lectures were published in Italian translation, by Giovanni Gherardini, in 1817. Rusconi similarly appended observations by Schlegel to his translations of* Romeo and Juliet, The Tempest, *and* Othello — *which, together with* Julius Caesar, *make up the first volume of his 'Complete Shakespeare', in which* Macbeth *is the first play.*

The English translation of Schlegel below is based on that of John Black, revised by A.J.W. Morrison (London: Henry G. Bohn, 1846), but has here been revised again to represent in English what Verdi read in Italian.

This is how one of the best German critics expresses himself about *Macbeth*:

Of *Macbeth* I have already spoken once in passing, and who could exhaust the praises of this sublime work? Since *The Eumenides* of Aeschylus, nothing so grand and terrible has ever been written. The witches are not, it is true, infernal divinities, and are not intended to be: they are ignoble and vulgar instruments of hell. A German poet[1], therefore, went strangely astray, when he sought to give them tragic dignity and transformed them into mongrel beings, a mixture of fates, furies and enchantresses. No man can lay hand on Shakespeare without bearing the penalty of his audacity: the bad is radically odious, and to endeavour to ennoble it, is to violate the laws of propriety. Hence, in my opinion, Dante, and even Tasso, have been much more successful in their portraiture of daemons than Milton. Whether the age of Elizabeth still believed in ghosts and witches, is a matter of perfect indifference for the justification of the use which in *Hamlet* and *Macbeth* Shakespeare has made of popular traditions. No superstition can be preserved and diffused through many centuries and among diverse people without having a foundation in human nature; and on this the poet builds. He calls up from their hidden abysses that dread of the unknown, that secret presage of a dark side of nature and of a world of spirits. In this manner he is in some degree like both the portrayer and the philosopher of superstition; that is, not like the philosopher who denies and turns it into ridicule, but what is still rare among men, like a thinker who distinctly exhibits its origin in so many opinions at once so disagreeable and yet so natural. If Shakespeare had ventured to make arbitrary changes in these popular traditions, he would have forfeited his right to them, and his most ingenious inventions would have seemed mere idle fancies. His picture of the witches has a certain magical quality: he has created for them a particular language, which, although composed of the usual elements, still seems to be a collection of formulae of incantation. The accumulation of rhymes, and the rhythmus of the verse, form, as it were, the hollow music of the nocturnal dances of these tenebrous beings. He has been abused for using the names of disgusting objects; but who has ever imagined that the magic kettle of the witches was filled with agreeable aromatics? That would be kin, as the poet says, to desiring that hell should give good counsel. These repulsive things, from which the imagination shrinks, are here emblems of the hostile powers which ferment in nature's breast; and the repugnance of our senses is outweighed by the mental horror. With one another the witches discourse like women of the very lowest class; for this was the class to which witches were ordinarily supposed to belong: when, however, they address Macbeth they assume a loftier tone: their predictions, which they either themselves pronounce, or allow their apparitions to deliver, have all the obscure brevity, the majestic solemnity of oracles, such as have ever spread terror among mortals. We here see that these enchantresses are merely instruments; they are governed by invisible spirits, or the operation of such great and dreadful events would be above their sphere. With what intent did Shakespeare assign the same place to them in his play, which they occupy in the history of Macbeth as related in the old chronicles? A monstrous crime is committed: Duncan, a venerable old man, and the best of kings, is, in defenceless sleep, under the hospitable roof, murdered by his subject, whom he has loaded with honours and rewards. Natural motives alone seem inadequate to explain such a deed, or the perpetrator must have been portrayed as the blackest and most hardened of villains. Shakespeare wished to exhibit a more sublime picture: he portrayed a noble but ambitious hero, yielding to a deep-laid hellish temptation, and in whom all the crimes to which, in order to secure the fruits of his first crime, he is impelled by necessity, cannot altogether eradicate the stamp of native heroism. Duncan's death is fully Macbeth's responsibility; but what is more hateful about it falls on the heads of those who instigated the horrid action. The first idea comes from those beings whose whole activity is guided toward wickedness. The witches surprise Macbeth in the intoxication of glory, after a battle in which he was victorious; they dazzle his eyes by exhibiting to him as the work of fate a vision of splendours that he can attain by a path of crime; and they gain credence for their words by the immediate fulfilment of an earlier prediction. The opportunity of murdering the King immediately offers; Lady Macbeth conjures her husband not to let it slip. She urges him on with a fiery eloquence, which has at command all those sophisms that can throw a false splendour over such a crime; and Macbeth, not master of himself, commits it in a tumult of fascination. Repentance immediately follows, nay even precedes the deed, and the stings of conscience leave him rest neither night nor day. But he is now fairly entangled in the snares of hell; truly frightful is it to behold that same Macbeth, who once as a warrior could spurn at death, now that he dreads the prospect of the life to come, clinging with growing anxiety to his earthly existence the more miserable it becomes, and pitilessly removing out of the way whatever to his dark and suspicious mind seems to threaten danger. Although we may abhor his actions, we cannot refuse to compassionate the state of his mind. We lament the ruin of his noble qualities; and nevertheless we admire even in his last defence the struggle of a brave will with a cowardly conscience.

It seems that the Destiny of the ancients rules again in this tragedy. From the very first scene, a supernatural influence manifests itself; and the first event to which it gives rise inevitably draws all the other events in its train. Here, in particular, are those ambiguous oracles which, by their literal fulfilment, deceive those who confide in them. Yet more enlightened views than those of paganism inspired this work. The poet wished to show that the conflict of good and evil in this world can only take place by the permission of Providence, which converts the curse that individual mortals draw down on their heads into universal blessings.

At the close, the poet distributes retribution to all his characters with an accurate measure. Lady Macbeth, who of all the participators in the king's murder is the most guilty, is thrown by the terrors of her conscience into a state of incurable bodily and mental disease. She dies unlamented by her husband, with all the symptoms of despair. Macbeth is still found worthy to die the death of a hero on the field of battle. The noble Macduff, his country's liberator, is allowed the satisfaction of saving his country by punishing with his own hand the tyrant who had murdered his wife and children. Banquo, the object of Macbeth's jealousy, by an early death atones for the ambitious curiosity which prompted his wish to know his glorious descendants; but as he preserved his mind pure from the evil suggestions of the witches, his name is blessed in his race, destined to enjoy for a long succession of ages that royal dignity which Macbeth could only hold for his own brief life. In the progress of the action, this tragedy is altogether the reverse of *Hamlet*: it strides forward with terrible rapidity from the first catastrophe (Duncan's murder) to the ending; and all designs are scarcely conceived but they are put into action.

In every feature of this vigorous design we see an energetic age, in the hardy North which breeds men of iron. The precise duration of the action cannot easily be ascertained: several years perhaps, according to the history; but we know that to the imagination the most crowded time appears always the shortest; and what has here been compressed into so narrow a space — not merely external events, but the very minds of the dramatic personages — is truly prodigious.

It is as if the drags were taken from the wheels of time, and they rolled along without interruption in their descent. Nothing can equal this picture in its power to excite terror. We need only allude to the murder of Duncan, the phantom dagger that hovers before the eyes of Macbeth, the vision of Banquo at the feast, the nocturnal entry of Lady Macbeth, walking in her sleep. Such scenes stand alone; only Shakespeare could have conceived them: and if they were more often played in the theatre, the Tragic Muse would be compelled to count the head of Medusa among her attributes.

Rusconi's excerpt ends at this point, but the notice in the Ricordi libretto of Macbeth *(see below) includes a paraphrase of what follows in Schlegel: 'I wish merely to point out as a secondary circumstance the prudent dexterity of Shakespeare, who could still contrive to flatter a king by a work in every part of whose plan nevertheless the poetical views are evident. James the First drew his lineage from Banquo . . .' etc.. Whoever its author may have been — Maffei seems a likely candidate — he evidently knew more of Schlegel than what appears in Rusconi.*

1. Schiller, whose adaptation of *Macbeth* was first performed at Weimar in 1800. Goethe, the stage director and designer of this famous production, also worked over the text. In this version, Macbeth was 'a consistently noble figure, a guiltless victim of fate, which was personified by the three witches, played by men in classic robes', with songs 'suggestive of Greek odes'. The Schiller *Macbeth* was published in 1801, and Andrea Maffei's Italian translation of it in 1863. AP.

The Preface in the Ricordi Libretto

Translated by Andrew Porter

As early as spring 1848, Ricordi's printed 'standard' libretto of Macbeth *included this preliminary note:*

Macbeth, Duncan's general, returning from a war in which he distinguished himself, fighting the rebels and the King of Norway, was in the intoxication of his glory surprised by witches who dazzled his eyes with a vision, presented as a prophecy, of grandeur which he could attain to only by a criminal path. Prompted by his wife, he did not delay to stain himself with blood of the best of kings and that of a friend; he mounted the throne using the heads of a thousand victims as his footstool; but he found on the battlefield and beneath Macduff's sword his deserved punishment.

Shakespeare took the idea of his play from the Scottish chronicles that tell of the general's meeting with the witches. Taking advantage of history, like an imaginative poet, he had these extraordinary beings predict the future with the majestic solemnity that is found in all oracular pronouncements and cloaks the truth beneath the aspect of the miraculous. 'Beware Macduff', the sorceresses intimate, indicating the plot that they would see woven against a gallant soldier who does not tolerate Macbeth's triumph. 'Thou mayst be bloody, ferocious, no man born of woman will harm thee' they intone to his ear, meaning that he will fall at the hand of a man not born but ripped from the

Frontispiece for the first piano-vocal score, 1847. (Photo: Royal Opera House Archives)

maternal womb; and, at last, they promise him, 'Thou shalt be glorious and invincible until thou seest Birnam Wood rise up and come against thee', indicating by that a shrewd martial device of his foes, who would use the branches of the forest as a screen for a numerous force. But Shakespeare had another political intent: to flatter James I. The son of the unhappy Mary Stuart traced his origin from Banquo and was the first to unite the three crowns of England, Scotland and Ireland; and therefore we see him pass with the visible sign of this triple power in the magic procession of the cavern, and he is promised a long series of successors.

Yet there is a section of the public that, while not supposing that tragic dignity is compromised by the spectre of Ninus or of the daughter of Aristodemus, considers Lemurs and Lamias the unworthy fantasies of an uncivilised nation's drama. Whether the men of Elizabeth's age believed in spirits and magic or not is a question quite irrelevant to the use the English poet made of them. Certainly no superstition could maintain itself and be diffused through many centuries if it did not have a foundation in the human heart; and it was to this that the poet directed himself. From the abysses he evoked the fear of the unknown, the secret presentiment of a mysterious part of nature, of an invisible world around us. For him, the witches are instruments governed by invisible spirits; by themselves they would not be able to rise to the sphere whence they influence events no less grand than terrible.

These preliminary observations seem worth making, because there are some — those whose passion for reason blinds them, as a modern critic has put it, to the intelligence of poetic reason — who do not wish to be persuaded that a kind of poetry such as that of *Macbeth* arises from the 'miraculous' (the 'miraculous' of Shakespeare's times as of ours, and as of those of the greatest masters of antiquity) and becomes absurd if it is derived from any sources other than contemporary beliefs and popular traditions.[1]

---

1. Hilary Gatti ('Shakespeare nei teatri milanesi dell'ottocento', *Biblioteca di Studi Inglesi*, 12 [Bari: Adriatica, 1968], 19) considers that these comments reveal a detailed knowledge of the Shakespearean tragedy, and in the original English, as well as a knowledge of the political situation in which the drama was written, and regards the comments on the witches as the best to be found in all of nineteenth-century Italy. Unfortunately, he attributes the authorship of this prefatory note to Piave. AP.

Piave's Intended Preface for the 1847 Libretto

Translated by Andrew Porter

Francesco Maria Piave to Giovanni Ricordi   *Venice, January 28, 1847*

Here, dear Ricordi, you have the signed declaration, and forgive me if I forgot to send it sooner on *carta bollata* [officially-stamped paper].

You will also find herewith attached the preface which I ask you also to let Lanari have, so that it can also be placed at the front of the Florence edition, and I am sure you will not fail to insert it in your own. It is indispensable for a full understanding of our treatment [of Shakespeare's play]. Farewell. Doubtless you will let me have some copies of this libretto of mine . . .

To the Readers

Edward the Confessor was on the throne of England when, toward the middle of the eleventh century, good King Duncan ascended that of Scotland. Times were difficult, because Scotland was internally racked by the revolts of its turbulent thanes (barons) and frequently assailed on its borders by the peoples of Denmark and Norway. King Duncan, finding himself incapable of quelling and rebuffing these internal and foreign enemies, entrusted the task to Macbeth, his valorous captain. The latter, seconded by Banquo, attained the objective and, not satisfied with the honours and rewards imparted to him by his king, dared to aspire to the royal power. To this aspiration the Scottish laws lent support, for they stipulated that, if the King should die leaving no sons of age, the crown should pass to the next of kin. Macbeth was that, and Duncan, being of an advanced age, had but two young children, Malcolm and Siward. Matters were at this stage when Duncan, by royal decree, named his first-born, Malcolm, as his successor. Then Macbeth, who thus saw his every legitimate hope for the succession vanish, waxed indignant and decided to obtain criminally that which would no longer become his by law; he conspired with the thanes his friends, among whom were Banquo and Macduff, and one night, when King Duncan, in the seventh year of his reign, was a guest at Inverness, Macbeth's castle, Macbeth, impelled to it also by his ambitious wife, murdered him. Malcolm fled into England, to Edward, Siward into Ireland, and Macbeth, having hastened to Scone, had himself crowned there as King of Scotland. Once the sceptre was his, he took to upholding his usurpation with all manner of harassment, and, having become suspicious even of his accomplices, he had Banquo murdered; and, as Macduff had succeeded in escaping him, he had his children and wife killed. In this wise he reigned for all of 17 years, at the end of which Malcolm, having obtained from King Edward 10,000 English soldiers, with the support of the thanes incited by Macduff and of the Scottish peoples weary of Macbeth's tyrannous oppression, conquered him, killed him, and recovered the hereditary throne.

So much is history. The later chronicles and national traditions, from which the immortal Shakespeare derived the subject of the present tragedy, which I have been so bold as to arrange in operatic form, accompany these facts with strange and fabulous circumstances, such as those of the witches. 'Shakespeare', as the celebrated G. Nicolini so admirably says, 'made the witches ministers of Hell in an enterprise destined to sacrifice innocence and ruin the guilty one himself; thus managing somehow to save the honour of the

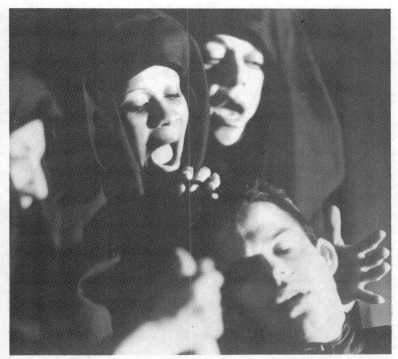

Omar Ebrahim as Macbeth with the witches, in Richard Jones' production, Scottish Opera's Opera-Go-Round, 1987. (Photo: Thorburn)

human race, and reducing within the bounds of the terrible what would otherwise have been ghastly and unbearable, and lending grandeur and solemnity to an action which, of itself, was only atrocious.'

Since, besides, he was writing in the days of James I, Banquo's descendant, he therefore was pleased to portray him innocent, whereas the histories prove he was an accomplice of the usurper Macbeth.

This much it was incumbent upon me to bring to the reader's attention for his better understanding of the present work.

Leo Nucci as Macbeth in Claude d'Anna's 1986 film of the opera. (Photo: Unitel)

Macbeth

Opera in Four Acts by Giuseppe Verdi

Text by Francesco Maria Piave
after William Shakespeare

English translation by Jeremy Sams

The first performance of *Macbeth* was at the Teatro della Pergola, Florence, on March 14, 1847. The first performance in America was at Niblo's Garden, New York, on April 24, 1850. The first performance in Britain was at the Theatre Royal, Manchester, on October 2, 1860. The opera was revised for Paris and first performed there, in French, at the Théâtre Lyrique on April 21, 1865. The first performance of the 1865 version (without the full 1865 ballet) in Britain was at Glyndebourne on May 21, 1938 and, in the United States, at the 44th Street Theatre, New York, on October 24, 1941.

This performing translation was made for the first production of the opera by English National Opera at the London Coliseum on April 5, 1990: the British stage première of the 1865 version complete with ballet.

The layout and scene divisions follow the revised libretto of 1865, established by Luigi Baldacci in *Tutti i libretti di Verdi* (Garzanti, 1975). The stage directions are from the score, and are literal translations which are not part of the ENO translation or production. The numbers in square brackets refer to the Thematic Guide.

CHARACTERS

Duncano	Duncan	*King of Scotland*	*silent*
Macbeth	Macbeth ⎫	*Generals of the King's Army*	*baritone*
Banco	Banquo ⎭		*bass*
Lady Macbeth	Lady Macbeth	*Wife of Macbeth*	*soprano*
Dama di Lady Macbeth	Gentlewoman	*Attending on Lady Macbeth*	*mezzo-soprano*
Macduff	Macduff	*Scottish Nobleman, Thane of Fife*	*tenor*
Malcolm	Malcolm	*Son to Duncan*	*tenor*
Fleanzio	Fleance	*Son to Banquo*	*silent*
Medico	A Doctor		*bass*
Domestico di Macbeth	A Servant to Macbeth		*bass*
Sicario	A Murderer		*bass*
Araldo	A Herald		*bass*
Ecate*	Hecate	*Goddess of the Night*	*silent*

Witches, Messengers of the King, Scottish Noblemen and Refugees, Murderers, English Soldiers, Bards*, Spirits of the Air, Apparitions.

The action takes place in Scotland, mainly in Macbeth's castle.
At the beginning of Act Four, it takes place on the Borders of Scotland and England.

* *1865 version only*

Pauline Tinsley as Lady Macbeth, Netherlands Opera, 1985. (Photo: Jaap Pieper)

Act One

Scene One. *A wood. Three groups of witches appear, one after the other, amidst lightning flashes and peals of thunder.*
Chorus of introduction.

WITCHES
I

Welcome sisters, it is late.   Che faceste? dite su!

II

Drink the cup of malice.   Ho sgozzata un verro.

I

                And hate.   E tu?

III

Let the poisoned chalice say   M'è frullata nel pensier
How to hurt the sailor's wife   La mogliera d'un nocchier:
Who is standing in our way.   Al dimòn la mi cacciò . . .
She denies the cult of Hell.
Let us conjure up a curse,
Let us conjure up a spell.
For her husband is a sailor on the sea;   Ma lo sposo che salpò
We will show her how malicious we can   Col suo legno affogherò.
   be.

I

We will blow the seas around . . .   Un rovaio ti darò . . .

II

We will run his boat aground . . .   I marosi io leverò . . .

III

Then the sailor will be drowned . . .   Per le seche lo trarrò.

A drum is heard.

ALL

I hear drumming. Who is near?   Un tamburo! Che sarà?
He is coming! Macbeth is here!   Vien Macbetto. Eccolo qua!

The groups of witches join into one, and dance in a circle.

ALL

Now we whirl in mazy motion   Le sorelle vagabonde
Round the world and round the ocean.   Van per l'aria, van sull'onde,
We describe a magic circle   Sanno un circulo intrecciar
On the sea and through the sky.   Che comprende e terra e mar.

Scene Two. *Macbeth and Banquo. The witches.*
Scene and duet.

MACBETH

Strange that this glorious day is drowned   Giorno non vidi mai sì fiero e bello!
   in darkness!

BANQUO

Yet blazing with sunlight.   Né tanto glorioso!

MACBETH
seeing the witches

                Oh, Heavens!   Oh, chi saranno
Who are these?   Costor?

61

BANQUO

Yes, who are you? Are you of this world	Chi siete voi? Di questo mondo,
Or are you from another?	O d'altra regïone?
Tell me how to address you. I'd	Dirvi donne vorrei, ma lo mi vieta
call you women	
But your beards contradict me.	Quella sordida barba.

MACBETH

What would you tell us?	Or via, parlate!

WITCHES
in prophetic tones

I

Hail to Macbeth, the great Thane of Glamis!	Salve, o Macbetto, di Glamis sire!

II

Hail to Macbeth, the new Thane of Cawdor!	Salve, o Macbetto, di Caudor sire!

III

Hail to Macbeth, who will soon be King!	Salve, o Macbetto, di Scozia re!

Macbeth trembles.

BANQUO
quietly to Macbeth

Why are you trembling at these happy tidings?	Tremar vi fanno così lieti auguri?

to the witches

You do not speak to me, you godless creatures.	Favellate a me pur, se non v'è scuro,
Tell me all you can see; what is my future?	Creature fantastiche, il futuro.

WITCHES

I

Banquo!	Salve!

II

Banquo!	Salve!

III

Banquo!	Salve!

I

Not so great as Macbeth and yet much greater!	Men sarai di Macbetto e pur maggiore!

II

He will be King, but you are twice as blessed!	Non quanto lui, ma più di lui felice!

III

For you will number Kings among your children!	Non re, ma di monarchi genitore!

ALL

Honour to Banquo and Macbeth!	Macbetto e Banco vivano!
Hail to you both in life and death!	Banco e Macbetto vivano!

They vanish.

MACBETH

They've gone!...   Vanîr!...

pensively

Your children will be kings of Scotland.   Saranno i figli tuoi sovrani.

BANQUO

And you will reign here before them.   E tu re pria di loro.

BANQUO AND MACBETH

Strange revelations!   Accenti arcani!

Scene Three. *Enter the King's messengers. Macbeth and Banquo.*

MESSENGERS

Hail, Macbeth! Your great royal master   Pro Macbetto! il tuo signore
Has proclaimed you Thane of Cawdor.   Sir t'elesse di Caudore.

MACBETH

The Thane of Cawdor is still alive!   Ma quel sire ancor vi regge!

MESSENGERS

No! The traitor, he has paid the   No! percosso della legge
Price of treason with his head.   Sotto il ceppo egli spirò.

BANQUO
to himself, in horror and awe

(God protect me! The witches spoke the   (Ah, l'inferno il ver parlò!)
    truth!)

MACBETH
quietly to himself, as if amazed

A double prophecy comes to fruition   [2] Due vaticini compiuti or sono...
And feeds the fire of my fierce ambition...   Mi si promette dal terzo un trono...
Why do I suffer with secret yearning?   Ma perché sento rizzarmi il crime?
My brain is teeming with thoughts of   Pensier di sangue, d'onde sei nato?...
    murder...
Though fate has shown me the crown I   Alla corona che m'offre il fato
    long for,
I cannot grasp it in my hand.   La man rapace non alzerò.

BANQUO
to himself

How they delight him, these mystic   Oh, come s'empie costui d'orgoglio,
    voices.
He dreams of power and his heart   Nella speranza d'un regio soglio!
    rejoices.
You must be wary of evil spirits.   Ma spesso l'empio Spirto d'averno
Their honeyed words are designed to   Parla, e c'inganna, veraci detti,
    deceive you.
For they will curse you and they will leave   E ne abbandona poi maledetti
    you,
Doomed to the burning fires of Hell.   Su quell'abisso che ci scavò.

MESSENGERS

(He seems unhappy to hear these tidings.   (Perché si freddo n'udì Macbetto?
Why is mistrust written on his face?)   Perché l'aspetto — non serenò?)

All slowly leave.

Scene Four. *The witches return.*

Witches' Chorus — Stretta of the Introduction.

WITCHES

Now they are leaving us! We'll meet again,	S'allontarnarono! — N'accozzeremo
When we hear the dreadful roar of thunder.	Quando di fulmini — lo scroscio udremo.
Now they are leaving us, now we must fly! . . .	S'allontarnarono, — fuggiam! . . . s'attenda
Their fate will be known at the next witches' sabbath.	Le sorti a compiere — nella tregenda.
Now we await the return of Macbeth.	Macbetto riedere — vedrem colà,
He'll learn the secrets of life and of death.	E il nostro oracolo — gli parlerà.
We fly, we fly!	Fuggiam, fuggiam!

They leave.

Scene Five. *A hall in Macbeth's castle, with other rooms leading off it. Lady Macbeth enters, reading a letter.*

Scena and Cavatina.

LADY MACBETH

'I met them on the very day of my triumph . . .	'Nel dì della vittoria io le incontrai . . .
I stood in amazement at what I heard;	Stupito io n'era per le udite cose;
Messengers from King Duncan came to hail me Thane of Cawdor. Thus the witches' first prophecy was fulfilled.	Quando i nunzi del Re mi salutaro Sir di Caudore, vaticinio uscito Dalle veggente stesse
But mark this, their second was that I would be King.	Che predissero un serto al capo mio.
Keep these secrets locked in your heart. Farewell.'	Racchiudi in cor questo segreto. Addio.'
Yes, you are ambitious.	Ambizioso spirto
But are you ruthless? I know you long for greatness,	Tu sei, Macbetto . . . Alla grandezza aneli,
But do you dare to steal it?	Ma sarai tu malvagio?
All roads to glory are paved with	Pien di misfatti è il calle
Dark deeds of evil; woe to the man who walks them,	Della potenza, e mal per lui che il piede
If he does not tread firmly or if he falters!	Dubitoso vi pone, e retrocede!
Hurry! I'll help you to do the deed! [3a]	Vieni! t'affretta! accendere
And raise the fire inside you!	Ti vo' quel freddo core!
I will provide all the strength you need;	L'audace impresa a compiere
I will be here to guide you.	Io ti darò valore;
The time has come; you must ascend the [3b] throne.	Di Scozia a te promettono
It was foretold; it is yours alone . . .	Le profetesse il trono . . .
Don't falter, don't hesitate, accept it!	Che tardi? accetta il dono,
Rise up and take the throne!	Ascendivi a regnar.

Scene Six. *A Servant and Lady Macbeth.*

SERVANT

His Royal Highness is coming here this evening.	Al cader della sera il Re qui giunge.

LADY MACBETH

The King? My husband with him?	Che di'? Macbetto è seco?

64

SERVANT

Macbeth is with him, Of that I am certain.	Ei l'accompagna. La nuova, o donna, è certa.

LADY MACBETH

Let us accord the King a right royal welcome.	Trovi accoglienza quale un Re si merta.

The servant leaves.

Scene Seven. *Lady Macbeth alone.*

LADY MACBETH

So Duncan will be here? . . . Here? . . . At our mercy? Assist me, you spirits of carnage and corruption, Who drives us bloodless mortals to death and destruction. Let night fall around us and shroud our deeds in darkness. The knife must not bear witness nor know whose heart it is defiling.	Duncano sarà qui? . . . qui? . . . qui la notte? Or tutti sorgete, — ministri infernali, Che al sangue incorate, — spingete i mortali! Tu, notte, ne avvolgi — di tenebra immota; Qual petto percota — non vegga il pugnal.

Scene Eight. *Macbeth and Lady Macbeth.*

Scene and March.

MACBETH

My noble lady!	Oh donna mia!

LADY MACBETH

Great Cawdor!	Caudore!

MACBETH

The King will soon be with us.	Fra poco il Re vedrai.

LADY MACBETH

When will he leave?	E partirà?

MACBETH

Tomorrow.	Domani.

LADY MACBETH

Let him not see the dawn of that tomorrow.	Mai non ci rechi il sole un tal domani?

MACBETH

My lady?	Che parli?

LADY MACBETH

You understand me? . . .	E non intendi? . . .

MACBETH

Completely, completely!	Intendo, intendo!

LADY MACBETH

Well, then?	Or bene?

MACBETH

What if the deed miscarries?	E se fallisse il colpo?

LADY MACBETH

You will not fail . . . if you are steadfast.	Non fallirà . . . se tu non tremi.

Sounds of rejoicing are heard, gradually approaching.

The King!   Il Re!

Music in the distance is heard from within.

Now we must greet him and make him   Trovi accoglienza quale un Re si merta.
welcome here.

They leave.

Scene Nine. *Rustic music, getting ever closer, announces the King's arrival. He processes by, accompanied by Banquo, Macduff, Malcolm, Macbeth, Lady Macbeth and entourage.*

Scene Ten. *Macbeth and a Servant.*

Gran scena and duet.

MACBETH
to a servant

Go and inform my lady that she should   Sappia la sposa mia che, pronta appena
tell me
When my nightly drink is ready,   La mia tazza notturna,
That a bell should be sounded. Do as I bid   Vo' che un tocco di squilla a me lo avvisi.
you.

The servant leaves.

Scene Eleven. *Macbeth alone.**

MACBETH

What is this that I see?! Is it a dagger?   Mi si affaccia un pugnal?! L'elsa a me volta?
If you are not a dream, then I will grasp   Se larva non sei tu, ch'io ti brandisca . . .
you . . .
You've vanished . . . but still I see you!   Mi sfuggi . . . eppur ti veggo! A me
You run away from me, but still point   precorri
The way, the course my racing thoughts   Sul confuso cammin che nella mente
Are destined to follow! . . . A dreadful   Di seguir disegnava! . . . Orrenda
nightmare!   imago!
See how your blade is bathed with   Solco sanguigno la tua lama irriga! . . .
bright streams of crimson! . . .
But now I see it's nothing. It was a   Ma nulla esiste ancor. Il sol cruento
figment
Of my black imagination, which has   Mio pensier le dà forma, e come vera
deceived me
By presenting as truth feverish visions.   Mi presenta allo sguardo una chimera.
Now is the time when night   Sulla metà del mondo
Has murdered half of nature; now the   Or morta è la natura; or l'assassino
assassin
Glides with the grace of a ghost through   Come fantasma per l'ombre si striscia,
the darkness,
Now is the time when witches perform   Or consuman le streghe i lor misteri.
their evil.
Motionless earth, do not echo to my   Immobil terra! a' passi miei sta'
footsteps . . .   muta . . .

A bell is heard tolling.

It's decided . . . the bell will be my   È deciso . . . quel bronzo, ecco, m'invita!
signal!
Pray the King does not hear it! It is a   * Non udirlo, Duncano! È squillo eterno
knell
And it will summon his soul to Heaven   Che nel cielo ti chiama o nell'inferno.
or to Hell.

He enters the King's chamber.

---

* This scene and duet should be sung with low and sinister voices, except for three phrases asterisked to be sung with an open voice.

Scene Twelve. *Lady Macbeth entering slowly, alone.*

LADY MACBETH

Now the whole world is sleeping ... Ah,
someone's sighing!
The owl sings with him as echo to his
parting!

Regna il sonno su tutti ... Oh, qual
lamento!
Risponde il gufo al suo lugubre addio!

MACBETH
from within

Who's there?

Chi v'ha?

LADY MACBETH

I hope that he was not awakened
Before the fatal blow!

Ch'ei fosse di letargo uscito
Pria del colpo mortal?

Scene Thirteen. *Lady Macbeth. Macbeth, hesitant and appalled, with a dagger in his hand.*

MACBETH

Now it is over!   [4]   Tutto è finito!
He goes up to Lady Macbeth, and asks quietly

Did you not hear it, a mournful sigh,
A strange unearthly shrieking?

Fatal mia donna! un murmure,
Com'io, non intendesti?

LADY MACBETH

I only heard the night owl cry ...
And then I heard you speaking.

Del gufo udii lo stridere ...
Testé che mai diceste?

MACBETH

Speaking?

Io?

LADY MACBETH

I thought I heard you calling me.

Dianzi udirti parvemi.

MACBETH

While I was up there?

Mentre io scendea?

LADY MACBETH

Yes! Yes!

Sì! Sì!

MACBETH

But in the other bedroom,
Who's in there?

Di'! nella stanza attigua
Chi dorme?

LADY MACBETH

His son, the prince ...

Il regal figlio ...

MACBETH
looking at his hands

What a sight, oh what a dreadful sight!   *   O vista, o vista orribile!

LADY MACBETH

You do not have to see it ...

Storna da questo il ciglio ...

MACBETH

In sleep his pages said their prayers,
Murmuring 'Heaven protect me'.
I could not couple my voice to theirs,
Somehow all sound had left me.
I could not say that last 'Amen'.
My voice could not be heard.

Nel sonno udii che oravano
I cortigiani, e: 'Dio
Sempre ne assista,' ei dissero;
'Amen' dir volli anch'io,
Ma la parola indocile
Gelò sui labbri miei.

LADY MACBETH

It's madness! | Follie!

MACBETH

Ah, why was I forbidden, then, | Perché ripetere
To speak that holy word? | Quel 'Amen' non potei?

LADY MACBETH

Enough, this madness will vanish | Follie, follie che sperdono
At the first light of day. | I primi rai del dì.

MACBETH

A voice spoke within me, unearthly and [5a] Allor questa voce m'intesi nel petto:
hollow:
'Your nightmare has started, but worse is | Avrai per guanciali sol vepri, o Macbetto!
to follow!
You murdered him sleeping, so sleep you | Il sonno per sempre, Glamis, uccidesti!
have murdered!
And you, Thane of Cawdor, will not sleep | Non v'è che vigilia, Caudore, per te!
again!'

LADY MACBETH

But what of the voices you should have [5b] Ma, dimmi, altra voce non parti d'udire?
been hearing?
'Macbeth is ambitious, but he is a coward: | Sei vano, o Macbetto, ma privo d'ardire:
His work is not finished, he dare not | Glamis, a mezz'opra vacilli, t'arresti,
complete it.
The heart of a baby, a vain, boastful boy.' | Fanciul vanitoso, Caudore, tu se'.

MACBETH

Like angels with wings made of vengeance [6] Com'angeli d'ira vendetta tuonarmi,
and thunder,
The King will be praised to the Heavens | Udrò di Duncano le sante virtù.
above.

LADY MACBETH
to herself

(See how this noble spirit has turned to | (Quell'animo trema, combatte, delira . . .
cowardice and madness . . .
Where is he now, the hero, the lionheart | Chi mai lo direbbe l'invitto che fu?)
I loved?)

to Macbeth

Now make haste! Take back the dagger . . . | Il pugnal là riportate . . .
Smear the guards while they are | Le sue guardie insanguinate . . .
sleeping . . .
Let the blood proclaim them guilty. | Che l'accusa in lor ricada.

MACBETH

Back in there? . . . I will not go back! | Io colà? . . . non posso entrar!

LADY MACBETH

I will do it. | Dammi il ferro.

She wrests the weapon from Macbeth's grasp and enters the King's chamber.

Scene Fourteen. *Macbeth alone. A loud knocking at the castle gates.*

MACBETH

Now every sound | Ogni rumore
Seems to reproach me! | Mi spaventa!

He looks at his hands; frightened.

Look at my hands! *	Oh, questa mano!
All the waters of the oceans	Non potrebbe l'Oceano
Could not wash this blood away!	Queste mani a me lavar!

Scene Fifteen. *Lady Macbeth and Macbeth.*

LADY MACBETH
reentering

Look! My hands are just as bloody;	Ve'! le mani ho lorde anch'io;
But I'll quickly wash them clean.	Poco spruzzo, e monde son.
Then the deed will be forgotten . . .	L'opra anch'essa andrà in oblio . . .

More knocking is heard.

MACBETH

Do you hear? There's someone there!	Odi tu? raddoppia il suon!

LADY MACBETH

Quick! We must seem above suspicion.	[7] Vien! Vieni altrove! ogni sospetto
You must find your former courage.	Rimoviam dall'uccisor;
So remember your position,	Torna in te! fa' cor, Macbetto!
Yes, remember what you are.	Non ti vinca un vil timor.

MACBETH

I'll ignore the thoughts of murder	Oh, potessi il mio delitto
Which are gnawing at my brain!	Dalla mente cancellar!
I will shake him from his slumber	Deh, sapessi, o Re trafitto,
And the King will wake again.	L'alto sonno a te spezzar!

Lady Macbeth drags Macbeth away.

Scene Sixteen. *Macduff and Banquo.*

Scena and sextet. First finale.

MACDUFF

I must rouse the King; he bade me wake him early:	Di destarlo per tempo il Re m'impose:
And it is late already:	E di già tarda è l'ora.
Wait for me here, worthy Banquo.	Qui m'attendete, o Banco.

He goes into the King's chamber.

Scene Seventeen. *Banquo alone.*

BANQUO

Oh, what a night of horrors!	Oh, qual orrenda notte!
Nightmarish voices screaming in the darkness,	Per l'aër cieco lamentose voci,
Voices of death and of evil.	Voci s'udian di morte.
The owl was hooting; it prophesied disaster,	Gemea cupo l'augel de' tristi auguri,
And somehow all the world seemed to be trembling . . .	E della terra si sentì il tremore . . .

Scene Eighteen. *Macduff and Banquo.*

MACDUFF
entering in a state of great agitation

Oh horror! Oh horror! Oh horror!	Orrore! Orrore! Orrore!

BANQUO

But what is wrong?   Che avvene mai?

MACDUFF
troubled

          There, inside,   Là dentro
You must see with your own eyes ...   Contemplate voi stesso ... io dir nol
  I cannot say it! ...   posso! ...
          Banquo rushes into the King's chamber.
Wake up, wake up! ... Hurry, everybody,   Correte! ... Olà! ... tutti accorrete! tutti!
  hurry!
This is treason! This is murder! This is   Oh delitto! oh delitto! oh tradimento!
  treason!

Scene Nineteen. *Macbeth, Lady Macbeth, Malcolm, Lady Macbeth's Gentlewoman and Servants enter hurriedly. Macduff and Banquo.*

LADY MACBETH

Who's causing this commotion?   Qual subito scompiglio!

BANQUO
coming out, in alarm

          It is disaster!   Oh noi perduti!

ALL

Alas, what is it? Tell us what has   Che fu? parlate! che seguì di strano?
  happened!

BANQUO
in horror

The King is dead, the noble King is   È morto assassinato il Re Duncano!
  murdered!

There is consternation.

ALL

Hell is gaping in horror and terror   [8] Schiudi, inferno, la bocca ed inghiotti
And its great jaws will swallow all   Nel tuo grembo l'intero creato;
  creation;
God in Heaven has seen the assassin   Sull'ignoto assassino esecrato
And the burning fire of vengeance will fall   Le tue fiamme discendano, o ciel.
  on his head.
Hear our prayer, merciful father in   O gran Dio, che ne' cuori penètri,
  Heaven,
Father, look into our hearts we beseech   Tu ne assisti, in te solo fidiamo;
  you;
Grant us guidance to brighten our   Da te lume, consiglio cerchiamo
  darkness,
Let us tear down the veil of night, let us see A squarciar delle tenebre il vel!
  the light!
Let your anger fall like thunder, let it roll in L'ira tua formidabile e pronta
  rage and terror;
Let the villain shake in wonder as your   Colga l'empio, o fatal punitor;
  vengeance falls on his head;
He'll be branded for treason,   E vi stampi sul volto l'impronta
Just as Cain was the first man to strike   Che stampasti sul primo uccisor.
  his brother dead.

Act Two

Scene One. *A room in the castle. Macbeth lost in thought, followed by Lady Macbeth.*

Scena and aria.

LADY MACBETH

Why do you spurn me and why do I	Perché mi sfuggi, e fiso
Always find you deep in sad reflection?	Ognor ti veggo in un pensier profondo?
The dead cannot return to life! The witches	Il fatto è irreparabile! Veraci
Were speaking the truth, for you are King now.	Parlâr le malïarde, e Re tu sei.
Since Duncan's eldest son has fled to England,	Il figlio di Duncan, per l'improvvisa
The world presumes him guilty	Sua fuga in Inghilterra,
Of his father's ghastly murder. What can prevent you?	Parricida fu detto, e vuoto il soglio
The throne is yours!	A te lasciò.

MACBETH

You have forgotten the witches	Ma le spirtali donne
And the face of the future — the House of Banquo . . .	Banco padre di regi han profetato . . .
When will his children reign as King?	Dunque i suoi figli regneran? Duncano
Was it	
For them that Duncan was murdered?	Per costar sarà spento?

LADY MACBETH

He and his son	Egli, e suo figlio
Are both still alive . . .	Vivono, è ver . . .

MACBETH

For the moment,	Ma vita
But they will not live forever!	Immortale non hanno . . .

LADY MACBETH

That's true, nor will they!	Ah sì, non l'hanno!

MACBETH

More blood must flow; we have work to do, my lady!	Forz'è che scorra un altro sangue, o donna!

LADY MACBETH

But how, and when?	Dove? Quando?

MACBETH

The blow must fall tonight.	Al venir di questa notte.

LADY MACBETH

But this time will you waver in your purpose?	Immoto sarai tu nel tuo disegno?

MACBETH

Banquo! You will be King, but not in this world.	Banco! l'eternità t'apre il suo regno . . .

He rushes off.

Scene Two. *Lady Macbeth alone.*

LADY MACBETH

Daylight is fading; fire in the firmament [9] La luce langue, il faro spegnesi
Flickers and falters, drowned by the   Ch'eterno corre per gli ampî cieli!
    darkness!
Night will provide the shroud that we long   Notte desiata provvida veli
    for,
Blackness will hide all the dark deeds   La man colpevole che ferirà.
    we do.

spoken

Bloodshed on bloodshed!   Nuovo delitto!

resolved

       But we must do it!   È necessario!
What we have started must be completed.   Compiersi debbe l'opra fatale.
To the departed, power means nothing;   Ai trapassati regnar non cale;
Sing them a 'requiem', bid them farewell.   A loro un 'requiem', l'eternità.

in rapture

Power is the spur which urges us on,   O voluttà del soglio!
The crown is all we can dream of!   O scettro, alfin sei mio!
Every human longing,   Ogni mortal desìo
Every desire will find its release in you.   Tace e s'acqueta in te.
The time is coming when death will strike   Cadrà fra poco esanime
The man who would be King.   Chi fu predetto re.

Scene Three. *A park. In the distance, Macbeth's castle.*

Chorus of Murderers.

MURDERERS

I

Who told you to join us here?   Chi v'impose unirvi a noi?

II

Macbeth gave orders.   Fu Macbetto.

I

        What did he say?   Ed a che far?

II

Banquo is to die today.   Deggiam Banco trucidar.

I

When, and where? . . .   Quando? . . . dove? . . .

II

       We'll wait with you.   Insiem con voi.
He and his son will soon be here.   Con suo figlio ei qui verrà.

I

All is well then, you may stay.   Rimanete, or bene sta.

ALL

See how soon the sun has left the sky. [10] Sparve il sol . . . la notte or regni
Does it know that men are doomed to   Scellerata, — insanguinata.
    die?
Not a soul will see the bloody sight.   Cieca notte, affretta e spegni
Death comes quicker at the dead of   Ogni lume in terra e in ciel.
    night.
We must hide now . . . for the time is   L'ora è presso! . . . or n'occultiamo,
    near;
Safe in silence we await them here.   Nel silenzio lo aspettiamo,

72

Tremble, Banquo, for the end is nigh.	Trema, o Banco! — nel tuo fianco
First you see a flash of steel, then you die!	Sta la punta del coltel!

They leave.

Scene Four. *Banquo and Fleance.*

Gran scena.

BANQUO

Quickly, son, we must hurry! . . .	Studia il passo, o mio figlio . . .
escape this terrible	usciam da queste
Darkness . . . Strange apprehensions,	Tenebre . . . un senso ignoto
Dark, nameless premonitions,	Nascer mi sento in petto,
Fill my heart with foreboding and with	Pien di tristo presagio e di sospetto.
suspicion.	

Black is the night, as black as death,	[11] Come dal ciel precipita
Dark, gloomy clouds surround me!	L'ombra più sempre oscura!
On such a dismal night as this	In notte ugual trafissero
Duncan met his doom.	Duncano, il mio signor.
Thousands of phantoms fill my brain	Mille affannose immagini
And wrap their shrouds around me.	M'annunciano sventura,
My darkest fears grow darker still,	E il mio pensiero ingombrano
As ghostly visions rise from the tomb.	Di larve e di terror.

They vanish into the park. Banquo's voice is heard offstage.

My son, now we are done for . . . they have	Ohimè! . . . Fuggi, mio figlio! . . . oh
betrayed us!	tradimento!

Fleance crosses the stage, pursued by a murderer.

Scene Five. *A magnificent hall. A table sumptuously laid. Macbeth, Lady Macbeth, Macduff, Lady Macbeth's Gentlewoman, Ladies and Gentlemen of the Court.*

Second finale.

CHORUS

Long live the King!	Salve, o Re!

MACBETH

My noble comrades,	Voi pur salvete,
You are welcome to this meeting.	Nobilissimi signori.

CHORUS

Hail, my lady!	Salve, o donna!

LADY MACBETH

From the bottom	Ricevete
Of my heart, I thank you for this greeting.	La mercé de' vostri onori.

MACBETH

Each sits at his alloted place	Prenda ciascun l'orrevole
According to his station.	Seggio al suo grado eletto.
It is my honour to welcome you	Pago son io d'accogliere
To join our celebration.	Tali ospiti a banchetto.
My lady will sit next to me	La mia consorte assidasi
As fits a royal consort.	Nel trono a lei sortito,
Then she will lead the Brindisi;	Ma pria le piaccia un brindisi
We'll sing the hours away.	Sciogliere, a vostr'onor.

Your loving queen needs no further bidding.
You speak and I obey.

Al tuo regale invito
Son pronta, o mio signor.

CHORUS

Our joyous song will echo yours
Crowning this happy day.

E tu ne udrai rispondere
Come ci detta il cor.

Brindisi.

LADY MACBETH

Come fill your glasses
With wine and gladness;
Farewell to sadness,
Welcome delight.
Let anger fly away
With care and with sorrow;
Forget about tomorrow,
Be happy tonight.
The power of song
Will turn pain into pleasure,
And every wrong
Can be put to right.
So banish bitterness,
Anger and hatred;
Feasting is sacred
To joy and delight.

[12] Si colmi il calice
Di vino eletto;
Nasca il diletto,
Muoia il dolor.
Da noi s'involino
Gli odi e gli sdegni,
Folleggi e regni
Qui solo amor.
Gustiamo il balsamo
D'ogni ferita,
Che nova vita
Ridona al cor.
Cacciam le torbide
Cure dal petto;
Nasca il diletto,
Muoia il dolor.

ALL
repeat the refrain.

Scene Six. *The persons above. A murderer appears at a side door. Macbeth goes up to him.*

MACBETH
quietly

You have blood upon your face.

Tu di sangue hai brutto il volto.

MURDERER

It is Banquo's.

È di Banco.

MACBETH

The deed is done, then?

Il vero ascolto?

MURDERER

Yes.

Sì.

MACBETH

And his son?

Ma il figlio?

MURDERER

He has fled!

Ne sfuggì!

MACBETH

Heavens! . . . But Banquo?

Cielo! . . . e Banco?

MURDERER

Banquo is dead.

Egli morì.

Macbeth makes a sign to the murderer to leave.

Scene Seven. *The same persons as before, but without the murderer.*

LADY MACBETH
going up to Macbeth

You do not join in our chorus;
What has drawn you from our feasting? ...

Che ti scosta, o re mio sposo,
Dalla gioia del banchetto? ...

MACBETH

Banquo should be here before us.
He's the only lord that's missing
From the perfect royal circle
Of the finest in our Kingdom.

Banco falla! il valoroso
Chiuderebbe il serto eletto
A quant'avvi di più degno
Nell'intero nostro regno.

LADY MACBETH

He was coming here, he said.

Venir disse, e ci mancò.

MACBETH

I will take his place instead.

In sua vece io sederò.

Macbeth goes to sit down. Banquo's ghost, which only he can see, is seated there.

Oh God, who has done this?

Di voi chi ciò fece?

ALL

What is it?

Che parli?

MACBETH
to the ghost

How dare you
Accuse me! ... or shake your foul
Bloody hair in my face ...

Non dirmi,
Ch'io fossi! ... le ciocche cruente
Non scuotermi incontro ...

ALL
rising in fear

Macbeth is demented!
We'll leave him ...

Macbetto è soffrente!
Partiamo ...

LADY MACBETH

Don't leave us! ...
His fever is passing ...

Restate! ... Gli è morbo
fugace ...

quietly to Macbeth

What sort of man are you?

E un uomo voi siete?

MACBETH

A King and a brave one
If I have the courage to look on that
thing,
On that devil incarnate ... Look ...
There ... Don't you see it there?

Lo sono, ed audace
S'io guardo tal cosa che al demone istesso
Porrebbe spavento ... là ... là ... nol
ravvisi?

to the ghost

Your head's bowed and bloody, but still
you can shake it,
So tell me if the dead can still haunt the
living?

Oh, poi che le chiome scrollar t'è concesso,
Favella! il sepolcro può render gli uccisi?

The apparition vanishes.

LADY MACBETH
quietly to Macbeth

My love, this is madness!

Voi siete demente!

75

MACBETH

My eyes are my witness . . .   Quest'occhi l'han visto . . .

LADY MACBETH
calmly

Sit down and be happy! Unease and   Sedete, o mio sposo! Ogni ospite è tristo.
  misgiving
Are blighting the banquet!   Svegliate la gioia!

MACBETH
calmly

My friends, please forgive me   Ciascun mi perdoni:
For spoiling the evening. I beg you sing   Il brindisi lieto di muovo risuoni,
  with me,
To praise the noble Banquo, who should   Né Banco obliate, che lungi è tuttor.
  be by my side.

LADY MACBETH

Come fill your glasses   Si colmi il calice
With wine and gladness;   Di vino eletto;
Farewell to sadness,   Nasca il diletto,
Welcome delight.   Muoia il dolor.
Let anger fly away   Da noi s'involino
With care and with sorrow.   Gli odi e gli sdegni,
Forget about tomorrow,   Folleggi e regni
Be happy tonight.   Qui solo amor.
The power of song   Gustiamo il balsamo
Will turn pain into pleasure,   D'ogni ferita
And every wrong   Che nova vita
Can be put to right.   Ridona al cor.
Let's drink to Banquo,   Vuotiam per l'inclito
Peerless and valorous.   Banco i bicchieri!
Soldier of soldiers,   Fior de' guerrieri,
Our own fearless Knight.   Di Scozia onor.

ALL
repeat the refrain.

The ghost reappears.

MACBETH
in terror

No! Leave me, you devil! . . . Let all Hell   Va, spirto d'abisso! . . . Spalanca una
  be opened,   fossa,
To swallow this demon . . . His bones burn   O terra, l'ingoia . . . Fiammeggian
  within him!   quell'ossa!
His lifeblood is boiling; it spatters and   Quel sangue fumante mi sbalza nel volto!
  scalds me!
His eyes pierce my being like knives in   Quel guardo a me volto — trafiggemi il cor!
  my heart!

ALL

Macbeth has gone mad!   Sventura! terrore!

MACBETH

There's none brave as I am!   Quant'altri io pur oso!
I'll wrestle a tiger, stand up to a lion . . .   Diventa pur tigre, leon minaccioso . . .
Let armies attack me, you'll not see me   M'abbranca . . . Macbetto tremar non
  tremble.   vedrai,
Undaunted, I stand by my sword.   Conoscer potrai — s'io provi timor . . .
But I fear this monster: leave me!   Ma fuggi! deh, fuggi, fantasma tremendo!

76

My strength is returning!

The apparition vanishes.
La vita riprendo!

LADY MACBETH
quietly to Macbeth

(You shame us, my lord!)   (Vergogna, signor!)

MACBETH

It wants blood. The ghost demands it;	Sangue a me quell'ombra chiede
It will not be disappointed!	E l'avrà, l'avrà, lo giuro!
It is time to return to the witches,	Il velame del futuro
So the future will be known.	Alle streghe squarcierò.

LADY MACBETH
to Macbeth

You're a coward and your terror	Spirto imbelle! il tuo spavento
Has invented these phantoms.	Vane larve t'ha creato.
You cannot undo the murder;	Il delitto è consumato;
And the dead cannot return.	Chi morì tornar non può.

MACDUFF
to himself

He is haunted and tormented.	Biechi arcani! . . . s'abbandoni
My poor country, ruled by a madman.	Questa terra: or ch'ella è retta
In a Scotland ruled by tyranny,	Da una mano maledetta
Only evil can take command.	Viver solo il reo vi può.

ALL

He is haunted and tormented.	Biechi arcani! sgomentato
Ghostly visions drive him to madness.	Da fantasmi egli ha parlato!
My poor country, you are fallen;	Uno speco di ladroni
Thieves and madmen rule the land.	Questa terra diventò.

Renato Bruson and Renato Scotto in Elijah Moshinsky's production for the Royal Opera House, 1981. (Photo: Reg Wilson)

Act Three

Scene One. A dark cave. In the centre, a boiling cauldron. Thunder and lightning. Witches.

Chorus of introduction — Enchantment.

WITCHES

I

Three times the tom-cat has yowled its cry of love.	Tre volte miagola la gatta in fregola.

II

Three times the raven has howled from the skies above.	Tre volte l'upupa lamenta ed ulula.

III

Three times the porcupine has screamed in terror.	Tre volte l'istrice guaisce al vento.

ALL

Now is the moment.	Questo è il momento.
Approach, the time is come to shape our sorcery,	Su via! sollecite giriam la pentola,
To work our witchery, to mix our magic mysteries.	Mesciamvi in circolo possenti intingoli:
Sisters, to work, to work round the cauldron!	Sirocchie, all'opera! l'acqua già fuma,
Now let the devil's daughters	
Spice the boiling waters.	Crepita e spuma.

throwing ingredients into the cauldron

I

This toad and this pustule,	Tu, rospo venefico
The poison will speed the spell.	Che suggi l'aconito,
This wolf-bane, this hemlock	Tu, vepre, tu, radica
Were plucked as the evening fell.	Sbarbata al crepuscolo,
Come, bubble in our cauldron	Va', cuoci e gorgoglia
With all the heat of Hell.	Nel vaso infernal.

II

The tongue of a viper,	Tu, lingua di vipera,
The skin of a hairy bat,	Tu, pelo di nottola,
The blood of a monkey,	Tu, sangue di scimmia,
The tooth of a mangy cat,	Tu, dente di bòttolo,
Will boil and melt and liquify	Va', bolli e t'avvoltola
With foul and loathsome smell;	Nel brodo infernal.
Will posset and solidify	
With all the heat of Hell.	

III

The claw of a wolf-cub	Tu, dito d'un pargolo
Was torn from its mother's womb,	Strozzato nel nascere,
The jaw of a Tartar	Tu, labbro d'un Tartaro,
Was found in a mouldy tomb.	Tu, cuor d'un eretico,
Come, throw them in the cauldron	Va' dentro, e consolida
And leave to simmer well.	La polta infernal.
They'll cook and boil and turn to oil,	
With all the heat of Hell.	

dancing around it

By the evil spirits	E voi, Spirti
Of red and blue,	Negri e candidi,
All our spells	Rossi e ceruli,
Will be mixed together!	Rimescete!
In the hellish heat	Voi che mescere
Of our brew,	Ben sapete,
They will be fused	Rimescete!
And fixed for ever!	Rimescete!

Ballet. *The stage fills with spirits, devils, witches, who dance around the cauldron. They stop dancing and invoke Hecate. Hecate, goddess of the night and of sorcery, appears. All bow in respect, and regard the goddess in religious terror. Hecate tells the witches that she knows their works and the reason why they invoked her. She looks around her attentively. Hecate announces that the King, Macbeth, is coming to question the witches about his destiny, and that they must give him satisfaction. If the terrible visions which they conjure up for him to see prove too much for him, they must invoke the spirits of the air to revive him and give him back his strength. But they must not reveal the end which is in store for him. The witches listen respectfully to the goddess's commands. Hecate disappears amid thunder and lightning. The witches dance around the cauldron hand in hand.*

Scene Two. *Macbeth and the witches.*

Gran scena of the apparitions.

MACBETH
at the entrance to the cave, to one of his attendants

I approach them, but dread what they may tell me.	Finché appelli, silenti m'attendete.

approaching the witches

What work is this, you strange and secret women?	Che fate voi, misteriose donne?

WITCHES
solemnly

Its name may not be spoken.	Un'opra senza nome.

MACBETH

In the name of all fiendish deeds I beg you	Per quest'opra infernal io vi scongiuro!
To let me know my fate. And should the truth set	Ch'io sappia il mio destin, se cielo e terra
The universe at war, let it be spoken.	Dovessero innovar l'antica guerra.

WITCHES

Do you wish to hear it from our masters, The lords of the earth, or from our mouths?	Dalle incognite Posse udire lo vuoi, Cui ministre obbediam, ovver da noi?

MACBETH

Conjure up any force who has the power To reveal to me the secrets of the future.	Evocatele pur, se del futuro Mi possono chiarir l'enigma oscuro.

WITCHES

From the lowest and highest of regions, Let the spirits appear and assemble!	Dalle basse e dall'alte regioni, Spirti erranti, salite, scendete!

There is a clap of thunder: a helmeted head appears.

MACBETH

Tell me, o spirit . . .   Dimmi, o spirto . . .

WITCHES

He knows all your questions;   T'ha letto nel cuore;
Keep your counsel and listen in silence.   Taci, e n'odi le voci segrete.

APPARITION

'O Macbeth! O Macbeth! O Macbeth!   'O Macbetto! Macbetto! Macbetto!
You should beware of Macduff.'   Da Macduffo ti guarda prudente.'

MACBETH

The warnings confirm my suspicions!   Tu m'afforzi l'ascolto sospetto!
Let me ask you . . .   Solo un motto . . .

The apparition disappears.

WITCHES

He will not be questioned.   Richieste non vuole.
Here's a greater, more powerful spirit.   Eccon un altro di lui più possente.

Thunder: a young boy appears, covered in blood.

You must be silent and hear his secret   Taci, e n'odi le occulte parole.
message.

APPARITION

'O Macbeth! O Macbeth! O Macbeth!   'O Macbetto! Macbetto! Macbetto!
Do not flinch to be fearless and bloody,   Esser puoi sanguinario, feroce:
For no man born of woman can harm   Nessun nato di donna ti nuoce.'
you.'

The apparition vanishes.

MACBETH

Live Macduff, for I fear you no longer . . .   O Macduffo, tua vita perdono . . .

in a rage

No! . . . You must die to protect me   No! . . . morrai! sul regale mio petto
And your death will be a double shield.   Doppio usbergo sarà la tua morte!

Lightning and thunder strike: a young boy wearing a crown rises up, holding a sapling.

What do they mean, this lightning, this   Ma che avvisa quel lampo, quel tuono? . . .
thunder? . . .
Another boy, but crowned like a king.   Un fanciullo col serto dei Re!

WITCHES

Hush and listen!   Taci, ed odi.

APPARITION

'Be bold and be reckless;   'Sta d'animo forte:
For no mortal will conquer Macbeth   Glorïoso, invincibil sarai
Till you see Birnam Wood start to move   Fin che il bosco di Birna vedrai
And to march like an army of death.'   Ravviarsi, e venir contro te.'

It disappears.

MACBETH

Oh, happy news! By no magic power   Lieto augurio! Per magica possa
Can the wood be uprooted.   Selva alcuna giammai non fu mossa.

to the witches

But my kingdom, my throne, is it   Or mi dite: salire al mio soglio
threatened
By any of Banquo's sons?   La progenie di Banco dovrà?

80

Do not ask it!   Non cercarlo!

MACBETH

I have to! I have to,   Lo voglio! lo voglio,
Or my anger will turn upon you!   O su voi la mia spada cadrà.
The cauldron disappears into the ground.
Now the cauldron has vanished! But   La caldaia è sparita! perché?
  why?
The sound of bagpipes is heard from underground.*
Distant music. What magic is this?   Qual concento! Parlate! Che v'è?

WITCHES
I

Let us see you!   Apparite!

II

Let us see you!   Apparite!

III

Let us see you!   Apparite!

ALL

Then, like mists on the sea, you must   Poi qual nebbia di nuovo sparite.
  vanish.

Eight kings now begin to file past, one after another. Last comes Banquo, with a mirror in his hand.

MACBETH
to the first

Leave me, you look like Banquo's ghost;   Fuggi, regal fantasima,
My victims are all returning.   Che Banco a me rammenti!
Your crown fulminates with blinding   La tua corona è folgore,
  fire;
My brain and my eyes are burning!   Gli occhi mi fai roventi!
The first king disappears. The second king appears.
Leave me, dreadful vision, leave me now.   Via, spaventosa immagine,
Whose is the crown that bedecks your   Che il crin di bende hai cinto!
  brow?
The king disappears. Another king appears, then suddenly disappears.
Others arise to take his place . . .   Ed altri ancor ne sorgono? . . .
A third king . . . another . . . yet another.   Un terzo? . . . un quarto? . . . un quinto?
Another king appears, then another, then the sixth and the seventh; the eighth is Banquo, who holds a mirror in his hand.
The worst of all, the final king   O mio terror! . . . dell'ultimo
Carries a silver mirror,   Splende uno specchio in mano.
Showing a line of future kings,   E nuovi Re s'attergano
Stretching into eternity . . .   Dentro al cristallo arcano . . .
And Banquo is smiling horribly!   E Banco, ahi, vista orribile!
He mocks me and points them out to me.   Ridendo a me li addita?
Die, you repulsive villain!   Muori, fatal progenie!
Drawing his sword, he advances upon the ghosts, then stops.
Ah, you are dead already!   Ah, che non hai tu vita!
to the witches
But will they live?   Vivran costor?

WITCHES

They will live!   Vivranno!

---

* Verdi creates the sound of the 'cornamusa', the Italian not the Scottish instrument, with two oboes, six clarinets, two bassoons and a contra-bassoon.

MACBETH

Then I am done for!   Oh me perduto!

He faints.

WITCHES

He's fainted! . . . Come, healing spirits,   Ei svenne! . . . Aerei spirti,
Bring the suffering King back to his   Ridonate la mente al Re svenuto!
senses!

Scene Three. *The spirits gradually descend and, while they dance around Macbeth, the witches sing the following:*

Chorus and dance tune (Ballabile).

CHORUS

Come nymphs and sirens,   Ondine e Silfidi
On your wings of thistledown,   Dall'ali candide,
Soothe him with music,   Si quella pallida
And sing to him sweetly.   Fronte spirate.
Cradle this child in a   Tessete in vortice
Cocoon of harmony.   Carole armoniche,
Your magic powers   E sensi ed anima
Will revive him completely.   Gli confortate.

Spirits and witches disappear.

Scene Four. *Lady Macbeth, Macbeth and a herald.*

Scena and duet — Third finale.

MACBETH
reviving

Where am I? . . . They've vanished . . . Oh,   Ove son io? . . . fuggiro! . . . Oh, sia ne'
may the dreadful moment   secoli
Be cursed to eternal damnation!   Maledetta quest'ora in sempiterno!

HERALD

Her royal highness.   La regina.

MACBETH

(What?)   (Che?)

LADY MACBETH
entering

           You here   Vi trovo
At last! What happened?   Alfin! Che fate?

MACBETH

           I went to   Ancora
The witches once again.   Le streghe interrogai.

LADY MACBETH

           Their message?   E disser?

MACBETH

'Beware of Macduff.'   'Da Macduff ti guarda.'

LADY MACBETH

           What then?   Segui.

MACBETH

'You need not fear any man born of a   'Te non ucciderà nato da donna.'
woman.'

82

LADY MACBETH

Go on.

Segui.

MACBETH

'And none will defeat you 'til the day
Birnam Wood rises up against you.'

'Invitto sarai finché la selva
Di Birna contro te non mova.'

LADY MACBETH

What then?

Segui.

MACBETH

Then Banquo's line processed in royal
glory . . .
Before my eyes!

Ma pur di Banco apparvemi la stirpe . . .

E regnerà!

LADY MACBETH

It's falsehood!
Death to all members of the house of
Banquo!

Menzogna!
Morte e sterminio sull'iniqua razza!

MACBETH

Yes, death, and Macduff will not escape
us!
Death to his wife and children!

Sì, morte! Di Macduffo arda la rocca!

Perano moglie e prole!

LADY MACBETH

And Banquo's son, he must be found and
slaughtered!

Di Banco il figlio si rinvenga, e muoia!

MACBETH

A river of crimson blood will be flowing!

Tutto il sangue si sperda a noi nemico!

LADY MACBETH

Ah! You have found again your former
courage and spirit!

Or riconosco il tuo coraggio antico.

TOGETHER

Now is the hour of revenge and murder. [13]
Now let the earth shake with terror and
thunder.
Now let the world stand in silence and
wonder.
The earth will be stunned by the force of
our wrath.
Angels of death, and ministers of
vengeance,
Fate has appointed us as agents of
murder.
What we have started must be completed.
The hand of fate is far too strong.
The wheels of death go rolling on.
To vengeance! To vengeance!

Ora di morte e di vendetta,
Tuona, rimbomba per l'orbe intero,

Come assordante l'atro pensiero

Del cor le fibre tutte intronò.

Ora di morte, omai t'affretta!

Incancellabile il fato ha scritto:

L'impresa compier deve il delitto
Poichè col sangue s'inaugurò.

Vendetta! vendetta!

Act Four

Scene One. *A deserted place on the border between Scotland and England. In the distance, Birnam Wood. Men, women and children, refugees from Scotland. Macduff to one side, grieving.*

Chorus of Scottish refugees.

CHORUS

Land of torture, beloved mother,	[14] Patria oppressa! il dolce nome
Hear your sons and daughters cry,	No, di madre, aver non puoi,
For the children whom you love	Or che tutta a' figli tuoi
Are condemned to waste and die.	Sei conversa in un avel.
How the weeping and the mourning	D'orfanelli e di piangenti
Of the widows and the orphans	Chi lo sposo e chi la prole
Rises up with each new morning,	Al venir del nuovo sole
Vainly reaching for the sky.	S'alza un grido e fere il ciel.
Heaven hears our lamentation,	A quel grido il ciel risponde
Turning grief into an echo,	Quasi voglia impietosito
Which resounds through all creation.	Propagar per l'infinito,
Oh, my country, this vale of tears!	Patria oppressa, il tuo dolor.
Let the death knell ring through the nation.	Suona a morto ognor la squilla,
There is no one to speak against it,	Ma nessuno audace è tanto
For it echoes our desolation	Che pur doni un vano pianto
And embodies our deepest fears.	A chi soffre ed a chi muor.

Scena and aria.

MACDUFF

My children, my little children! That I should leave you	O figli, o figli miei! da quel tiranno
In the fangs of a tyrant; and your mother,	Tutti uccisi voi foste, e insiem con voi
That she should perish with you! . . .	La madre sventurata! . . . Ah, fra gli artigli
How could I leave	
My wife and children in the clutches of a tiger?	Di quel tigre io lasciai la madre e i figli?
Where was your loving father?	[15a] Ah, la paterna mano
He was not there to guard you,	Non vi fu scudo, o cari,
Safe from the heartless murderer,	Dai perfidi sicari
The bloody man who brought your death!	Che a morte vi ferir!
Fled far from home and hidden,	E me fuggiasco, occulto,
I could not run to you when I was bidden.	Voi chiamavate invano,
Oh, how could I desert you?	Coll'ultimo singulto,
You called me with your final breath.	Coll'ultimo respir.
Soon I will meet him face to face,	Trammi al tiranno in faccia,
And, God, if he escapes me,	Signore! e s'ei mi sfugge,
Then open up your arms,	Possa a colui le braccia
To forgive him, to grant him grace.	Del tuo perdon aprir.

Scene Two. *At the sound of a drum, Malcolm enters, at the head of many English soldiers.*

MALCOLM

What is this? What is this forest?	Dove siam? che bosco è quello?

CHORUS

Birnam Wood shall stand for vengeance!	La foresta di Birnamo!

MALCOLM

Let each man take up a tree,	Svelga ognuno, e porti un ramo,
And let the branches hide his face.	Che lo asconda, innanzi a sé.

to Macduff

Then revenge will bring you comfort.	Ti conforti la vendetta.

MACDUFF

Not enough . . . he has no children!	Non l'avrò . . . di figli è privo!

MALCOLM

If you love your mother country,	Chi non odia il suol nativo
Take up arms and march with me.	Prenda l'armi e segua me.

Malcolm and Macduff draw their swords.

ALL

Your country is calling,	[15b] La patria tradita
She begs you release her,	Piangendo ne invita!
From sorrow, from slavery,	Fratelli! gli oppressi
The curse of these times.	Corriamo a salvar.
The anger of Heaven	Già l'ira divina
Will fall on the tyrant;	Sull'empio ruina;
For destiny grows weary	Gli orribili eccessi
Of hearing his crimes.	L'Eterno stancâr.

Scene Three. *A room in Macbeth's castle, the same one as in Act One. It is night-time. A Doctor and Lady Macbeth's Gentlewoman.*

The Sleepwalking Scene (gran scena del sonnabulismo).

DOCTOR

Two nights we've watched and waited.	Vegliammo invan due notti.

GENTLEWOMAN

Tonight she will appear.	In questa apparirà.

DOCTOR

What was she saying	Di che parlava
When she was sleeping?	Nel sonno suo?

GENTLEWOMAN

I dare not	Ridirlo
Repeat it, I cannot tell you . . . there she	Non debbo ad uom che viva . . .
is! . . .	Eccola! . . .

Scene Four. *Lady Macbeth and the above. Lady Macbeth enters slowly, walking in her sleep and carrying a lamp.*

DOCTOR

And with	Un lume
A light in her hand?	Recasi in man?

GENTLEWOMAN

The lantern which we always	La lampada che sempre
Keep lit by her highness' bedside.	Si tiene accanto al letto.

DOCTOR

Her eyes are open	Oh, come gli occhi
And staring!	Spalanca!

GENTLEWOMAN

And yet see nothing!	E pur non vede.

Sylvia Sass in Philippe Sireuil's 1987 production for La Monnaie, Brussels. (Photo: La Monnaie)

Lady Macbeth puts down the lamp, and rubs her hands together, as if trying to remove something from them.

DOCTOR

She is wringing her hands.   Perchè sfrega le man?

GENTLEWOMAN

She tries to clean them.   Lavarsi crede!

LADY MACBETH

There's a stain here, and here's   [16a] Una macchia è qui tuttora . . .
   another . . .
Who will clean them? Their sins are   Via, ti dico, o maledetta! . . .
   scarlet! . . .
Listen . . . listen . . . now you must do it.   Una . . . due . . . gli è questa l'ora!
You're afraid . . . afraid to go in?   Tremi tu? . . . non osi entrar?
Not a soldier, but a coward.   [16b]Un guerrier così codardo?
Oh, it's shameful . . . Come on, take   Oh vergogna! . . . orsù, t'affretta! . . .
   courage! . . .
Who'd have thought it, that that old man   Chi poteva in quel vegliardo
Would have so much blood inside his   Tanto sangue immaginar?
   veins?

DOCTOR

What is this? . . .   Che parlò? . . .

LADY MACBETH

   The Thane of Fife once   Di Fiffe il Sire
Had a wife and little children? . . .   Sposo e padre or or non era? . . .
But where are they? . . .   Che n'avvenne? . . .

She looks at her hands.

   They are so filthy,   E mai pulire
They will be stained for evermore . . .   Queste mani io non saprò? . . .

GENTLEWOMAN AND DOCTOR

God in Heaven! . . .   Oh terror! . . .

LADY MACBETH

   Still I can smell them,   Di sangue umano
Foul and bloody . . . All of the perfumes   Sa qui sempre . . . Arabia intera
Of Arabia could not   Rimondar sì piccol mano
Make my hands smell sweet again.   Co' suoi balsami non può.
Alas! . . .   Ohimè! . . .

DOCTOR

She's sighing!   Geme?

LADY MACBETH

   Come, you must pull   I pani indossa
Yourself together! . . . Put on your   Della notte . . . Or via, ti sbratta! . . .
   nightgown! . . .
Banquo's dead and in his tomb.   Banco è spento, e dalla fossa
That which is dead cannot return to life.   Chi morì non surse ancor.

DOCTOR

Do you hear? . . .   Questo ancor? . . .

LADY MACBETH

   It's time for bed now . . .   A letto, a letto . . .
That we have done cannot be undone . . .   Sfar non puoi la cosa fatta . . .

Someone's knocking! . . . Macbeth, have courage,	Batte alcuno! . . . andiam, Macbetto,
Don't let your guilty face give you away.	Non t'accusi il tuo pallor.

GENTLEWOMAN AND DOCTOR

God forgive her sins, O Lord!	Ah, di lei pietà, Signor!

Scene Five. *A room in the castle. Macbeth.*
Scena and Aria.

MACBETH

Treachery! The exiles dare unite against me!	Perfidi! All'anglo contra me v'unite!
But the words of the spirits reassure me:	Le potenze presaghe han profetato:
'Do not flinch to be fearless and bloody,	'Esser puoi sanguinario, feroce:
For no man born of woman can harm you.'	Nessun nato da donna ti nuoce.'
No, Macbeth does not fear you, no, nor the callow	No, non temo di voi, né del fanciullo
Youth who commands you! All is in the balance;	Che vi conduce! Raffermar sul trono
War will strengthen my kingdom,	Questo assalto mi debbe,
Or destroy me completely . . . And yet my courage,	O sbalzarmi per sempre . . . Eppur la vita
The lifeblood of my being is draining from me!	Sento nelle mie fibre inaridita!

When you are old and full of tears,	[17] Pietà, rispetto, amore,
Who'll watch you when you are sleeping?	Conforto ai dì cadenti,
No one will soothe your empty years,	Non spargeran d'un fiore
Or lighten the load of death.	La tua canuta età.
Mourners may meet at your graveside,	Né sul tuo regio sasso
But you will not hear them weeping:	Sperar soavi accenti:
They will accuse you of murder	Sol la bestemmia, ahi lasso!
And spit upon your grave!	La nenia tua sarà!

WOMEN'S VOICES WITHIN

God in Heaven!	Ella è morta!

MACBETH

Who's shouting there?	Qual gemito?

Scene Six. *Lady Macbeth's Gentlewoman, and Macbeth.*
Scena and battle.

GENTLEWOMAN

	The queen,		È morta
My lord, is dead! . . .		La Regina! . . .	

MACBETH
with indifference and disdain

	Is life so important? . . .		La vita . . . che importa? . . .
Years of struggle for moments of glory;		È il racconto d'un povero idiota;	
Vain and futile, a meaningless story!		Vento e suono che nulla dinota!	

The gentlewoman leaves.

Scene Seven. *Chorus of soldiers and Macbeth.*

CHORUS OF MACBETH'S SOLDIERS

Quickly! Come quickly!   Sire! ah, Sire!

MACBETH

What news?... What has happened?   Che fu?... quali nuove?

CHORUS OF MACBETH'S SOLDIERS

Like an ocean the forest advances!   La foresta di Birna si muove!

MACBETH
astonished

So the fates have conspired to delude   M'hai deluso, presago infernale!...
me!...
Bring my weapons, my armour and my   Qui l'usbergo, la spada, il pugnale!
dagger!
Sound the trumpets! To death or on to   Prodi, all'armi! La morte o la gloria.
glory.

CHORUS OF MACBETH'S SOLDIERS

Sound the trumpets! To death or on to   Dunque all'armi! sì, morte o vittoria.
glory.

The sound of trumpets is heard from within. At the same time, the scene is transformed into a vast plain, surrounded by mountains and woodland. At the rear are English soldiers, who slowly advance, each carrying a branch in front of him.

Scene Eight. *Malcolm, Macduff and soldiers.*

MALCOLM

Throw down your branches and take your   Via le fronde, e mano all'armi!
weapons!
I will lead you!   Mi seguite!

Malcolm, Macduff and the soldiers leave.

To battle! To battle!   All'armi! All'armi!

The sounds of battle are heard off-stage.

Scene Nine. *Macbeth pursued by Macduff. Then a chorus of women.*

MACDUFF

At last, the butcher who has slain my   Carnfice de' figli miei, t'ho giunto.
children.

MACBETH

You were born of a woman.   Fuggi! Nato di donna
I'm not afraid of you.   Uccidermi non può.

MACDUFF

You are mistaken! They cut me   Nato non son; strappato
From my mother's womb!   Fui dal seno materno.

MACBETH

Heavens!   Cielo!

They brandish their swords and, fighting fiercely, leave the stage.

Scottish women and children enter, in distress.

CHORUS OF WOMEN

Death and destruction!   Infausto giorno!
May God protect our children!   Preghiam pe' figli nostri!
Now all is peace!   Cessa il fragor!

89

Final Scene. *Malcolm enters, followed by English soldiers, who drag on Macbeth's troops, whom they have taken prisoner. Macduff with other soldiers, bards and the people.*

Hymn of Victory — Finale.

MALCOLM

Victory!... Where is the villain,   Vittoria!... ove s'è fitto
Where is Macbeth?   L'usurpator?

MACDUFF

He's there, in all his glory.   Colà da me trafitto.
sinking on one knee to the ground
God save the King!   Salve, o Re!

CHORUS OF BARDS

God save the King!   Salve, o Re!
Macbeth, where is Macbeth,   [18] Macbeth, Macbeth ov'è?
Who dared to steal the crown?   Dov'è l'usurpator?
How soon the swift and mighty breath of   D'un soffio il fulminò
  Heaven
Struck the villain down.   Il Dio della vittoria.
to Macduff
We praise the fearless man   Il prode eroe egli è
Who did the fatal deed!   Che spense il traditor!
With honour he defended   La patria, il Re salvò;
King and country in their hour of need!   A lui onor e gloria!

CHORUS OF SOLDIERS

We praise the fearless man   Il prode eroe egli è
Who did the fatal deed!   Che spense il traditor!
With honour he defended   La patria, il Re salvò;
King and country in their hour of need!   A lui onor e gloria!

CHORUS OF WOMEN

Our prayers rise up to you,   Salgan mie grazie a te,
O God in Heaven above;   Gran Dio vendicator;
Your grateful people sing   A chi ne liberò
Their thanks in hymns of praise and   Inni cantiam di gloria.
  love.

MACDUFF

Now war has ceased, put your trust   S'affidi ognun al Re
In your victorious King!   Ridato al nostro amor!
Look forward to the peace   L'aurora che spuntò
And to the plenty that his reign will   Vi darà pace e gloria!
  bring!

MALCOLM

Now war has ceased, put your trust   Confida, o Scozia, in me;
In your victorious King!   Fu spento l'oppressor!
This victory will show   La gioia eternerò
The happy future that my reign will   Per noi di tal vittoria.
  bring!

The end of the opera.

Additional Scenes from the 1847 version

Some of the scenes and arias set in the first version of the opera were abandoned in the second, as readers may see from Harold Powers' article on the score. Here are the passages of the libretto which form no part of the second version. There is a tradition to include Macbeth's final aria in performances which are otherwise of the 1865 version. Although the big Act Three ballet with Hecate is often cut, note that the opening witches' chorus and the dancing and chorus of 'Ondine e Silfidi' form part of the 1847 version and were retained in the 1865 version.

Act Two

The end of Scene One.

MACBETH

Banquo! You will be King, but not in this world.	Banco! l'eternità t'apre il suo regno...

Macbeth rushes off.

Scene Two. *Lady Macbeth alone.*

Aria ('Trionfai!').

LADY MACBETH

It is done! We have triumphed, we have conquered.	Trionfai! Trionfai!
We can take the throne of Scotland.	Securi alfine premerem di Scozia il trono.
I defy the powers of darkness	Or disfido il lampo, il tuono,
To prevent us now.	Le sue basi a rovesciar.
The beginning was in evil,	Tra misfatti l'opra ha fine
Only evil can complete it.	Se un misfatto le faculta,
For the royal crown is nothing,	La regal corona è nulla,
If we do not grasp it firmly in our hands.	Se può in capo vacillar!

Act Three

End of Scene Three. *The witches' cave. Macbeth faints and the chorus and ballabile 'Ondine e silfidi' are performed.*

Scene Four. *Macbeth's aria ('Vada in fiamme').*

MACBETH
reviving

Where am I?... They've vanished!... Oh, may the dreadful moment	Ove son io?... Sparito!... Oh sia ne' secoli
Be cursed to eternal damnation!	Maledetta quest'ora in sempiterno!
Oh, Macbeth, time is flying,	Vola il tempo, o Macbetto,
And your power must be seen	E il tuo potere dèi per opre
In your deeds, not in your visions.	Affermar, non per chimere.
An inferno, a mighty earthquake	Vada in fiamme, e in polve
Will engulf him and destroy him!	Cada l'alta rocca di Macduffo!
All his children will taste my anger	Figli, sposa a fil di spada
And their blood will start to flow.	Scorra il sangue a me fatal.
Now my vengeance will roll like thunder,	L'ira mia, la mia vendetta
And resound through all creation.	Pel creato si diffonda,
Naked hatred is my salvation,	Come fiera il cor m'innonda,
For my spirit begins to grow.	Come l'anima m'assal.

Act Four

At the end of Scene Eleven, Macduff has fought Macbeth on stage and Macbeth has fallen mortally wounded.

Final Scene. *Macbeth's Death Scene ('Mal per me').*
Enter Malcolm, followed by English soldiers with Macbeth's troops as prisoners.

MALCOLM

Victory!... Where is the villain,
Where is Macbeth?

Vittoria!... ove s'è fitto
L'usurpator?

MACDUFF
pointing to Macbeth

He's there!

Trafitto!

MACBETH
He rises very slowly from the ground, dying:

I have sinned, for I have trusted in
The promptings of the devil!
So much bloodshed, so much heartache.
Heaven's vengeance on my life of evil!...
Now my heart is torn asunder;
Heaven's curse came down like thunder!
I perish... abandoned by earth and
  Heaven;
For this crown, all this for you!

Mal per me che m'affidai
Ne' pressagi dell'inferno!...
Tutto il sangue ch'io versai
Grida in faccia dell'Eterno!...
Sulla fronte maledetta
Folgorò la sua vendetta!
Muoio!... al Cielo... al mondo...
  in ira,
Vil corona! e sol per te!

He dies.

MACDUFF AND MALCOLM

Days of peace return to Scotland!
Noble Malcolm is our King.

Scozia oppressa omai respira!
Or Malcolmo è il nostro re.

CHORUS

Noble Malcolm is our King.

Or Malcolmo è il nostro re.

The end of the opera.

Discography *by David Nice*

Conductor	Leinsdorf	Sawallisch	Muti
Company/Orchestra	Metropolitan Opera	Vienna State Opera	Ambrosian Opera Ch New Philharmonia Orch
Date	1959	1964 (live recording)	1976
Macbeth	L. Warren	D. Fischer-Dieskau	S. Milnes
Lady Macbeth	L. Rysanek	G. Bumbry	F. Cossotto
Banquo	J. Hines	P. Lagger	R. Raimondi
Macduff	C. Bergonzi	E. Lorenzi	J. Carreras
Malcolm	W. Olvis	F. Lazaro	G. Bernardi
UK LP number	–	–	(EMI) EX 290385-3 (2)
UK tape number	–	–	(EMI) EX 290385-5 (2)
UK CD number	(RCA) GD84516 (2)	(Frequenz) 011-036 (2)	(EMI) CDS7 47954-8 (2)
US LP number	–	–	(Angel) EX 290385-3 (2)
US tape number	–	–	(Angel) EX 290385-5 (2)
US CD number	(RCA) 4516-2RG (2)	–	(Angel) CDS7 47954-8 (2)

Conductor	Abbado	Sinopoli	Chailly
Company/Orchestra	La Scala	Deutsche Oper, Berlin	Teatro Communale, Bologna
Date	1976	1981	1987
Macbeth	P. Cappuccilli	R. Bruson	L. Nucci
Lady Macbeth	S. Verrett	M. Zampieri	S. Verrett
Banquo	N. Ghiaurov	R. Lloyd	S. Ramey
Macduff	P. Domingo	N. Shicoff	V. Luchetti
Malcolm	A. Savastano	C.-H. Ahnsjö	A. Barasoda
UK LP number	—	(Philips) 412 133-1PH3 (3)	—
UK tape number	—	(Philips) 412 133-4PH3 (3)	—
UK CD number	(DG) 415 688-2GH3 (3)	(Philips) 412 133-2PH3 (3)	(Decca) 417 525-2DH2 (2)
US LP number	—	(Philips) 412 133-1PH3 (3)	—
US tape number	—	(Philips) 412 133-4PH3 (3)	—
US CD number	(DG) 415 688-2GH3 (3)	(Philips) 412 133-2PH3 (3)	(London) 417 525-2LH2 (2)

Selective Excerpts

Number	Artists	LP number	Tape number	CD number
Prelude	Karajan/BPO	(DG)413 544-1GX2 (2)	(DG) 413 544-4GX2 (2)	—
Witches' Chorus/Patria oppressa (original version)	Armstrong/Welsh National Opera Ch and Orch	(CFP) 414506-1	(CFP) 414506-4	—
Vieni! t'affretta!/La luce langue/Una macchia è qui	M. Callas	(EMI) EMX 2123 (*La luce* only)	(EMI) TC-EMX 2123 (*La luce* only)	(EMI) CDC7 47730-2
Vieni! t'affretta!/Una macchia è qui	A. Baltsa	(EMI) EL 270478-1	(EMI) EL 270478-4	(EMI) CDC7 47627-2
La luce langue/Una macchia è qui	J. Barstow	(TER) VIR 8307	(TER) ZCVIR 8307	(TER) CDVIR 8307
Come dal ciel precipita	P. Burchuladze I. Andresen (r. 1929) J. Morris	(Decca) 414 335-1DH (EMI) EX 290169-3 (3) (EMI) CDC7 49287-2	(Decca) 414 335-4DH	(Decca) 414 335-2DH
Ballet music	Gibson/SNO	(Chandos) ABRD 1032	(Chandos) ABTD 1032	(Chandos) CHAN 8739
Patria oppressa	Gardelli/ Ambrosian Ch LPO	—	(Decca) 417 177-4DA	(Decca) 421 309-2DÀ
Ah, la paterna mano	L. Pavarotti	—	—	(Decca) 417 304-2DA or (Decca) 417 570-2DH
	P. Domingo (live recording)	(EMI) EL 7498111	(EMI) EL 7498114	(EMI) CDC7 49112
Una macchia è qui	B. Nilsson (cond. Schippers) R. Crespin L. Price A. Millo	—	(Decca) 417 530-4DA	— (EMI) CDM7 69547-2 (RCA) RD 87016 (EMI) CDC7 47396-2
Pietà, rispetto, amore	B. Weikl S. Estes	—	—	(Acanta) 43327 (Philips) 416 818-2PH

Bibliography

⌐n of the 1865 score is not yet available, although David Lawton ⌐d a critical edition of the 1847 version.

⌐ent reference throughout the Guide to *Verdi's 'Macbeth': A Sourcebook* ⌐ited by David Rosen and Andrew Porter (W.W. Norton & Co./Cambridge UP, 1984) will have shown that this remarkable anthology is indispensable for a serious study of the opera. It contains the contemporary documentation about the opera's composition and performance, in the original and translation, and a series of papers given at the Danville Congress on *Macbeth* in 1977 by noted authorities on different aspects of the work. It concludes with reproductions of the complete 1847 libretto and the principal pages of the 1847 score that were revised or recomposed in 1865. The extracts from Schlegel and the Ricordi libretto introduction printed in this Guide have been reproduced from the *Sourcebook* with permission.

An introduction to Verdi's operas is admirably given in Julian Budden's *Verdi* in the Master Musician series (Dent, 1985) and there is a longer analysis in the first volume of his *The Operas of Giuseppe Verdi* (Cassell, 1984; currently out of print). David Kimbell's *Verdi in the Age of Italian Romanticism* (Cambridge UP, 1981) offers an extensive consideration of the opera, from the context of its composition, the score, and the impact of Shakespeare. On the other hand, the most interesting studies of Verdi and Romanticism in general are by Gary Tomlinson ('Italian Romanticism and Italian Opera: An Essay in their Affinities', *19th-Century Music*, 1986) and Piero Weiss ('Verdi and the Fusion of Genres', Journal of the American Musicological Society, 35, 1982). Daniela Goldin's important study of the libretto (in Italian) is included in *La vera fenice* (Einaudi, 1985).

The leading study of the staging of *Macbeth* as a play (not merely in the nineteenth century) is Dennis Bartholomeusz, *Macbeth and the Players* (Cambridge UP, 1969) and, of all the editions of the play, the Cygnet Classic edition may be recommended for the inclusion of many major essays and historic commentaries.

Contributors

Giorgio Melchiori is Professor of English in the University of Rome.

Harold Powers is Professor of Music at Princeton University, New Jersey, and works on Italian opera, the music of India and the history of Western music theory.

Michael R. Booth is Professor in the Department of Theatre of the University of Victoria, British Columbia.

Jeremy Sams is a composer, writer and translator, whose other opera translations include *The Magic Flute*.

David Nice, freelance writer and broadcaster, is the author of a forthcoming study of Richard Strauss (Omnibus, London).